100 SCIENTISTS

—WHO SHAPED— WORLD HISTORY

JOHN HUDSON TINER

sourcebooks
eXplore

Copyright © 2000, 2023 by Sourcebooks
Text by John Hudson Tiner
Cover design by Will Riley
Internal illustrations by AAARep/Geo Parkin
Cover and internal design © 2023 by Sourcebooks

Published by Sourcebooks eXplore, an imprint of Sourcebooks Kids
P.O. Box 4410, Naperville, Illinois 60567-4410
(630) 961-3900
sourcebookskids.com

Originally published in 2000 by Bluewood Books, an imprint of The Siyeh Group, Inc.

Cataloging-in-Publication Data is on file with the Library of Congress.

Source of Production: Versa Press, East Peoria, Illinois, USA
Date of Production: May 2023
Run Number: 5032109

Printed and bound in the United States of America.
VP 10 9 8 7 6 5 4 3 2 1

CONTENTS

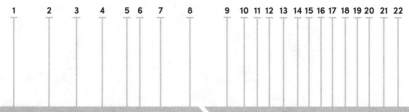

Timeline of Birthdates

580 BCE   **1700**

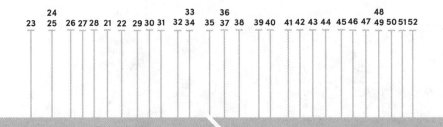

1706

1829

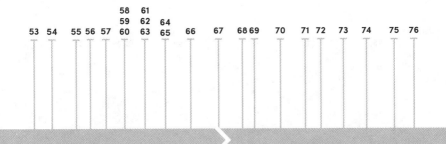

1830

1889

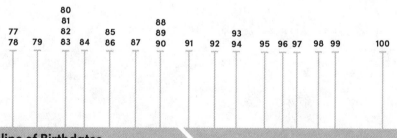

Timeline of Birthdates

1890   1942

INTRODUCTION

SCIENCE IS a process of gaining knowledge about the physical world. Before science can flourish, a society must be strong enough to give individuals the economic freedom to observe, experiment, and think. Although individuals with great minds might exist in very poor nations, their daily struggle to survive prevents them from pursuing their ideas. In addition to economic freedom, science requires intellectual freedom. Some cultures suppressed new ideas because of the fear of change. If it was possible to replace the Earth at the center of the universe with the Sun, as Copernicus theorized in the mid-1500s, then what was to prevent a king from being replaced from his position on the throne?

Science also requires that its practitioners make permanent records of their achievements. Scientists gain credit for their advances only by revealing them to the whole world. Only then can these achievements be studied and assessed by other scientists, who then determine their potential value and benefit. During the Middle Ages (400–1400 CE), European scientists were obsessed with producing synthetic gold. They kept their methods and discoveries secret. Those individuals may have made remarkable achievements, but because of their secrecy, they received no credit for their discoveries. In 1662, the first formal scientific body, the Royal Society of London, was established primarily to ensure that new learning was quickly communicated to the scientific community.

Throughout history, a breakthrough in one scientific field tended to cause a flurry of activity within the other branches of science. For that reason, clusters of important scientific achievements were attained during key historical periods. One period of great advancement occurred during the time of the ancient Greeks (580-200 BCE). Following the fall of Rome in 476 CE, Arab scientists kept alive the achievements of the Greeks while Europe fell into the decline of the Middle Ages. In the first scientific revolution, from 1450 to 1650, the founders of modern science introduced the idea of experimentation, or controlled observation, to gain insight into the physical world. During the next 250 years, scientists made several important advances; however, by the end of the nineteenth century, science seemed in danger of becoming stagnant. Then in the space of only ten years—from 1895 to 1905—the discovery of X-rays, radioactivity, and the theory of relativity paved the way for the great scientific and technological advances of the next hundred years.

This book contains short biographies of one hundred scientists who had a major impact on society and the world. The men and women in this book include physicians, naturalists, mathematicians, physicists, chemists, and individuals from several other disciplines. Each biography contains a brief personal history, but the larger focus is on the individuals' scientific contributions—breakthroughs and discoveries often made at great personal sacrifice and sometimes announced to a skeptical and disbelieving world.

Within these pages are the stories of the men and women whose hard work, brilliant thinking, and self-sacrifice cured deadly diseases, invented great tools of communication and methods of transportation, and uncovered many of the mysteries of space and time that had puzzled and even frightened people from the dawn of the human race.

The most famous idea in geometry was developed more than two thousand years ago by **PYTHAGORAS**—an ancient Greek scholar who believed in simple dress, humble possessions, and frequent self-examination.

Pythagoras was born on the island of Samos in the Aegean Sea. He traveled extensively in Egypt and visited Babylon in search of knowledge. About 530 BCE, he settled in Croton, a Greek colony in Southern Italy, and gained a following of disciples who came to be called the "Pythagoreans."

Pythagoras believed that the world is mathematical in nature. He applied mathematics to music and discovered that the sounds of stringed instruments are related in simple multiples to the lengths of their strings. If one string is held so the part that vibrates is one-half its original length, the sound emitted is an octave higher. Such findings about the mathematics of music, or "harmonics," remain important today.

Pythagoras also saw a mathematical

order in **astronomy**. He believed the planets orbit the Sun at intervals corresponding to the harmonic lengths of strings. He thought that the movement of the planets gives rise to a musical sound, the "harmony of the spheres." The notion of planetary music has not endured, but Pythagoras did correctly note that the morning star and the evening star are the same object. This star became known as "Aphrodite" to the Greeks and "Venus" to the Romans.

However, Pythagoras is best known for his contribution to **geometry**. He developed the **Pythagorean theorem**: the square of the length of the hypotenuse of a right triangle is equal to the sum of the squares of the lengths of its other two sides. The Egyptians employed this fact earlier, but Pythagoras understood the difference between an empirical rule of thumb and a rigorous mathematical proof.

One discovery, however, devastated Pythagoras and his followers. They believed the common whole numbers (1, 2, 3, 4, and so on) and the fractions formed by them (1/2, 1/3, 2/3, 1/4, 3/4, and so on) were sufficient to explain all of mathematics and nature. Yet they also found that the diagonal of a square cannot be expressed as the ratio of two numbers. No two whole numbers can be found such that the square of one is exactly twice the square of the other. This discovery caused an uproar among the Pythagoreans. They successfully suppressed the discovery for many years. With their mystical beliefs, the Pythagoreans were considered eccentric and even radical by their neighbors. Their political activities eventually resulted in the exile of Pythagoras. He fled to Megapontum, a Greek city in Southern Italy, where he died. None of his writings has survived, although his disciples recorded his beliefs and probably added to them.

Known as the father of modern medicine, **HIPPOCRATES** was the first person to separate medicine from superstition. Born on the Greek island of Cos, the son of a physician, Hippocrates dismissed the belief held by his contemporaries that diseases are caused by vengeful gods. Instead, he proposed that every sickness has a natural cause. "Find the cause," he said, "then you can cure the disease." By watching the symptoms of a disease and noting their severity, Hippocrates said, a doctor can state a prognosis for a particular patient by comparing his progress with the typical course of the same disease. Hippocrates began a school of medicine based on such rational ideas.

Another medical idea Hippocrates recognized was that a cure for one patient may not help another. He said, "One man's meat is another man's poison." Hippocrates also urged physicians to use simple remedies, such as healthy diet, plenty of rest, and clean surroundings. He said, "Nature often brings about a cure when doctors cannot." Should simple methods fail, and a patient is near

death, he suggested then that "desperate diseases require desperate remedies."

Hippocrates promoted what today would be called a good bedside manner with such statements as, "illness is sometimes stronger when a mind is troubled" and "some patients recover their health simply through their contentment with the goodness of the physician." He taught that doctors should serve their patients and follow honorable standards of conduct. During his time, a doctor was sometimes bribed to ensure that a patient died. A ruler might order a doctor to prepare poison to kill an enemy. Hippocrates said that a physician's duty is to the patient.

Hippocrates endorsed a pledge that is still affirmed by medical students when they become doctors. The **Hippocratic oath** contains guidelines for honorable conduct. The modern oath states in part, "I solemnly pledge myself to consecrate my life to the service of humanity; I will practice my profession with conscience and dignity, and the health of my patient will be my first consideration."

Although Hippocrates contributed much to the art of healing, little is known of his personal life. Historians believe he visited Egypt and studied medicine there; he then taught in various places, including Athens. Eventually he returned to his home on the island of Cos to begin his own medical school. A statue uncovered on Cos, believed to be of Hippocrates, shows a short man with a curly beard.

Hippocrates's sayings have survived because his students collected notes of his lectures and published books describing them. More than fifty books carry Hippocrates's name, and his writings are sufficient to justify his title of the **father of medicine**.

ARISTOTLE was a Greek philosopher, scientist, and educator. He was born in Macedonia, the son of a physician who personally served the king. When he was a young boy, Aristotle's father sent him to Athens to study at the **Academy of Plato**. Plato recognized in the seventeen-year-old Aristotle a great desire to learn; Aristotle remained at Plato's Academy for twenty years, first as a student and then as a teacher.

Upon Plato's death in 348 BCE, Aristotle left Athens and returned to Macedonia. For seven years, Aristotle served King Philip of Macedonia as the private tutor of his son, Alexander. The greatest thinker of the ancient world became the tutor to the individual who would become its greatest military leader, **Alexander the Great**. Student and teacher formed a strong bond of friendship. In 336 BCE, Alexander became king of Macedonia following the death of his father. He was twenty years old. He quickly set out to conquer the great empires of the world—and did so.

Aristotle returned to Athens and formed his own school, the Lyceum, where he continued his life's work. Aristotle made careful observations, collected specimens, and summarized and classified all existing knowledge of the physical world. His systematic approach became so influential that it later evolved into the basic scientific method employed in the Western world.

Aristotle's ideas applied not only to the physical world. During this time, he produced **treatises on logic**—considered to be his most important work—as well as those on metaphysics, physics, ethics, and natural sciences. In the latter subject, he was one of the first scientists to collect and systematically classify biological specimens. In politics, he suggested that the ideal form of government was a combination of democracy and monarchy.

In 323 BCE, the thirty-three-year-old Alexander the Great died of a fever in Babylon. With the death of his protector, Aristotle faced danger in Athens because of a long-standing rivalry between Athens and his native Macedonia. Consequently, Aristotle left Athens and went to live on an island in the Aegean Sea, where he died a year later.

After his death, many of Aristotle's notebooks were preserved in caves near his home. They were later brought to the great library at Alexandria in Egypt. Though they were used and valued by Islamic scholars, these works were lost or forgotten in Europe through the Dark Ages. Later they were reintroduced and have exerted a major influence on all of Western thought for many centuries.

EUCLID, a Greek mathematician, lived in the city of Alexandria, Egypt. He wrote his famous book on **geometry** in that great city of learning. Euclid's textbook, *Elements of Geometry*, has been in continuous use for more than two thousand years. Julius Caesar, Isaac Newton (see no. 20), George Washington, and Albert Einstein (see no. 72) all learned geometry from Euclid's book. Millions of high school students have studied elementary plane geometry, based on the first part of Euclid's presentation.

Euclid gave to science the understanding that gathering facts is not enough. The facts must be given in logical order, summarized, and systematized to build general principles. Euclid carefully planned the organization of his book. First, he collected everything known about the subject. He stated a number of definitions and basic truths, or "axioms." He arranged the rest of the book to follow logically, and he supplied missing proofs. Euclid developed his geometric conclusions from mathematical proofs based on the basic axioms and "postulates," or assumptions, that he listed at the beginning.

Euclid's fifth assumption was the parallel postulate: Through a point not on a given line, one and only one line can be drawn parallel to the given line. From the **parallel postulate** comes the result that the three interior angles of any triangle must total 180 degrees. The great mathematician **Carl Gauss** (see no. 35) tested this observation centuries later. He used powerful telescopes and precise surveying equipment to measure the angles of triangles several miles on a side. Within experimental error, the angles in each one totaled 180 degrees, in agreement with Euclid's geometry.

Still, the parallel postulate is merely an assumption. Mathematicians, including Gauss, have substituted alternate assumptions to see what occurs. Astronomers believe that some of these "non-Euclidean geometries" may have some application to the real world. For example, the mathematics governing neutron stars and black holes may be non-Euclidean.

Elements of Geometry is a comprehensive study of plane geometry, proportion, properties of numbers, and solid geometry. Within this book, Euclid's best-known single achievement is his proof that the number of prime numbers is infinite.

Euclid's most famous quote concerns a statement he made to **Ptolemy I**, king of Egypt and Libya. Ptolemy is supposed to have studied geometry under Euclid and found the exacting proofs to be a challenge. He asked for a simpler presentation. Euclid promptly replied, "There is no royal road to geometry."

As to Euclid's personal life, practically nothing is known. He probably studied at Athens before traveling to Alexandria. He wrote *Elements of Geometry* in Greek, and the book came to the scientists of the Renaissance in Latin by way of a translation from Arabic.

◆ Of the many ancient scientists, **ARCHIMEDES** was perhaps the most modern. He used mathematical concepts to investigate the physical world in a manner similar to Isaac Newton (see no. 20) and other scientists of the Enlightenment. After an education at Alexandria, Egypt, Archimedes returned to his home in Syracuse on the island of Sicily and served under the patronage of **Hieron II**. One of Archimedes's early accomplishments was the development of formulas for finding areas and volumes of spheres and cylinders. For an irregularly shaped curve, he represented the surface as small triangles or rectangles and summed their areas.

Archimedes built inventions with his own hands, quite unlike the other Greek philosophers. He is credited with designing **Archimedes' screw** for raising the level of water, which was applied to irrigating fields. His experiments with the lever resulted in his statement of the **law of simple machines**: the load times the distance the load moves, equals effort times the distance through which the effort is applied. Archimedes told Hieron II that with a place to stand and a long enough lever, he could move the world. Hieron challenged him to single-handedly drag a full barge out of the water. Archimedes attached a compound pulley, which he had invented, to the barge and succeeded in pulling it ashore.

A more difficult problem was Hieron's order to establish whether a new crown was made of pure gold. However, Archimedes solved the problem by finding a way to test the crown's density (its mass divided by its volume). He used the **law of buoyancy**, which he had discovered while in the bath: a submerged object is buoyed upward with a force equal to the weight of the water it displaces, which in turn depends on the volume of the water displaced.

Archimedes put the new crown on a balance with an equal mass of pure gold in the other pan. Then he submerged it in the water. If the pans balanced after they were submerged, the new crown must have the same density as the gold sample, proving that the crown was pure gold. When he realized he had the solution he shouted, "Eureka!" (I have found it!)

In the **Second Punic War**, Syracuse became allied with Carthage against the forces of the Roman Empire. With Archimedes's help, the people of Syracuse defended their city. He is credited with inventing the catapult and incendiary devices that helped the citizens keep the opposing Roman army at bay for three years. The city finally fell in 212 BCE, and the Romans stormed into the city. A Roman soldier came across a seventy-five-year-old man drawing figures in the sand. The old man scolded him for stepping on his figures. The soldier ran him through with a sword, not knowing he had killed the great scientist.

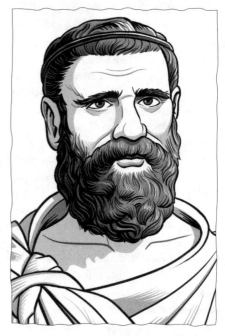

ERATOSTHENES grew up in Cyrene, a Greek town in northern Africa. He studied at Alexandria in Egypt and then at Athens, returning to Alexandria in 255 BCE to settle there. Eratosthenes produced writings on mathematics, astronomy, geography, history, and literary criticism. Such a record made him the logical scholar to be placed in charge of the library in Alexandria, a post he accepted in 240 BCE.

At that time, **Ptolemy III** ruled Alexandria and parts of Egypt. He ordered that all ships and caravans be searched for books, maps, or interesting documents to be copied. The library at Alexandria became a storehouse of the vast knowledge of the ancient world.

With the world's intellectual riches readily available to him, Eratosthenes compiled a map of the known world. It extended from the British Isles to Sri Lanka and included all the countries that bordered the Mediterranean Sea. It remained useful for two hundred years. He also realized that the Egyptian solar calendar was too short by one day every four years, causing the calendar to fall behind the seasons. He suggested adding an extra day every four years.

Eratosthenes is best known for **calculating the size of the Earth**, a conclusion he reached by using an ingenious method. Eratosthenes knew that the Sun is highest in the sky at noon on June 21, the summer solstice. At the special time, a vertical stick casts its shortest shadow. If the Sun is directly overhead, the stick casts no shadow at all. This occurs in Syene, a city south of Alexandria, where the Aswan Dam is located today. How did Eratosthenes reason that the Sun was directly overhead at Syene at this unique time? He knew from library information that at noon on June 21, sunlight shines directly down a deep well in Syene, and is reflected straight back up, thus showing the Sun is directly overhead. Using simple geometry, Eratosthenes showed that a 7.2-degree angle existed between Alexandria and Syene. A 7.2-degree angle corresponds to one-fiftieth of a circle. The distance between Syene and Alexandria was well traveled and known to be 5,000 stadia. So, Eratosthenes calculated the Earth to be 50 × 5,000 stadia, or about 250,000 stadia. This is remarkably close to the modern accepted circumference of the Earth, about 24,540 miles.

Eratosthenes showed that the Earth is a much larger place than the Greeks had imagined. This disturbed the Greeks because it made the known world seem too small in comparison. They rejected Eratosthenes's value in favor of a smaller, incorrect one.

Despite his success as a scholar and writer, the latter part of Eratosthenes's life was tragic. He became blind and eventually starved himself to death at the age of eighty.

The Greek physician **GALEN** lived during the time when the Roman Empire dominated Europe. The Romans emphasized public health in their approach to medicine. They built aqueducts to carry fresh water, arranged for sewers to conduct away waste, and built public baths for personal cleanliness. For all its successes, this approach had limitations. It failed to provide cures for individual illnesses and did not take into account anatomy. Galen helped address the shortcomings of Roman medicine.

After studying medicine at Pergamum in Asia Minor and Corinth in Greece, Galen then traveled to Alexandria, Egypt. The great library and museum located there contained two complete human skeletons. Galen believed that "a physician needs to study the body, as an architect needs to follow a plan." Since Roman law forbade cutting into human cadavers, Galen dissected pigs, goats, and apes. He described what he saw in careful detail. He learned much, but not everything he found in the animals held true in the human body. For example, a network of blood vessels below the brain is common in animals, but the pattern is not found in human beings.

Galen learned more about **human anatomy** when he returned to Pergamum in 157 CE to serve as physician at a school for gladiators. Galen repaired the wounded fighters and learned human anatomy firsthand.

Galen relocated to Rome in 162 CE and demonstrated the benefits of his acquired knowledge. **Eudemus**, a well-known physician, suffered a mild paralysis in his right hand. After local doctors failed to help him, Eudemus sent for the new doctor in town. Galen asked Eudemus about recent injuries. Eudemus had been thrown from a chariot and injured his neck. Galen knew that nerves from the fingers connected to the spinal column. Rather than treating the man's fingers, Galen treated the nerves in Eudemus's neck. His patient completely recovered. With that success, **Marcus Aurelius**, the Roman emperor, commissioned Galen as his court physician.

During his lifetime, Galen wrote a large number of books and medical tracts, more than one hundred of which are known. His books contain a mixture of fact, opinion, and outright errors. He showed that arteries carry blood and not air but missed the important discovery that the heart is a blood pump.

Because of his monotheism (belief in one God), Galen's teachings found favor with medieval religious authorities. Galen's belief that disease results from an imbalance of four vital fluids, or **humors**, of the body was accepted for centuries. It was thought that doctors could restore a person to good health by **bloodletting** and bringing the four humors into balance. It was not until the 1700s that medical authorities exposed some of the fundamental errors of Galen's theories.

IBN SĪNĀ was the most accomplished physician between the time of the Roman Empire and the rise of modern science in the 1500s. Also known by his Latin name, **AVICENNA**, his influence extended throughout the Islamic world and in Western Europe of the Middle Ages. (Hakim is an Arabic word for a physician.)

Ibn Sīnā was born in what is now Uzbekistan but was at that time part of Persia. The home of his father, a tax collector, was the meeting place for people of learning. He grew up studying Islamic law, literature, and medicine.

At age seventeen, he cured King Mansor of Bukhara of an illness after other physicians had failed. In payment, Ibn Sīnā asked for use of the Royal Library. He served as the court physician until the fall of the kingdom in 999 CE. He then traveled widely, working during the day as a physician, and meeting at night with the bright minds of the area for philosophical and scientific discussions.

Ibn Sīnā settled in Hamadan in Iran on the main trade route between Tehran and Baghdad. As physician to several sultans, he enjoyed fame and a healthy income. While in Hamadan he wrote extensively. *The Book of Healing* is his largest work—an encyclopedia of medicine, natural science, logic, and philosophy. Ibn Sīnā brought skepticism to the study of alchemy, the belief that gold could be made from base metals such as lead.

The prince he served in Hamadan died in 1022. Ibn Sīnā then moved to Esfahan, in central Iran, where he completed *The Canon of Medicine*. In this book, he recounts the major achievements of the Greek and Roman physicians. He systematically listed 760 drugs and medical preparations. Ibn Sīnā recognized the contagious nature of tuberculosis and the role water can have

in spreading diseases. He was the first to describe the illness **meningitis**. In addition, he provided a detailed description of the parts of the eye.

In Esfahan, Ibn Sīnā served as physician to Ala al-Dawlah. While accompanying the prince on a military campaign to capture Hamadam, Ibn Sīnā took ill and died. His burial site in **Hamadan** eventually became a major visitor attraction.

After his death, Ibn Sīnā's works were translated into Latin and became available to European thinkers. His books served as the primary resource in medical schools for four centuries. Within fifty years after the invention of the printing press, *The Canon of Medicine* was printed fifteen times. His protocol is still the basis of modern clinical tests of the effectiveness of drugs. He showed that a drug must be used on a patient who has but one disease, it must prove effective in all or in most cases, and animal tests alone will not prove its effectiveness on humans.

◆ **NICOLAUS COPERNICUS** is famous for his statement that the Earth moves around the Sun—and not the other way around.

Copernicus was born in Torún, Poland, the son of a merchant. As a young man, he studied mathematics at the University of Kraków; he then went on to study astronomy, law, classics, and medicine at various universities in Italy. After obtaining a degree in canon law, Copernicus returned to Poland in 1506 to serve as private physician to his uncle, a Catholic bishop. In his spare time Copernicus also applied mathematics to **astronomy** to calculate planetary positions and predict the times of celestial events such as eclipses.

During this time, planetary calculations were made difficult by **retrograde,** or apparently backward looping, motions of the outer planets. Mars, Jupiter, and Saturn appeared to pause in their forward orbit and make a backward loop before going forward again.

Ptolemy, the ancient Greek astronomer, succeeded in explaining the backward loops by using a combination of small circles moving around larger circles. His complex system needed a total of seventy circles.

Copernicus agreed with the idea that planetary motion is circular, but he believed the Sun, and not the Earth, occupied the center of the planetary system. Putting the Sun at the center of the planets made calculations easier and reduced the number of circles.

Copernicus showed that retrograde motion occurred when the Earth overtook Mars or one of the other outer planets, causing it to fall behind. Copernicus worked out his system in full mathematical detail. He summarized his ideas in a short, hand-written manuscript, and sent it around to his friends and fellow scientists in 1530.

As time passed, Copernicus added to his manuscript. His confidence in his view of the planetary system was bolstered by new evidence. For example, during a period of about two years, Mars faded from a bright red object to a much dimmer one. The Earth-centered planetary system offered no explanation for this observation. However, Copernicus realized that if Mars and Earth both traveled around the Sun at different speeds, they would sometimes be close together and this would make Mars brighter. At other times, Earth and Mars would be farther apart and Mars would be dimmer.

Copernicus gathered his evidence for the **Sun-centered planetary system**. At the time, government and religious officials did not encourage original thought for fear that new ideas would create unrest. Copernicus hesitated for thirteen years before taking the dangerous step of sending *On the Revolutions of the Celestial Spheres* to the printer. The first copy of the book arrived on May 24, 1543, as he lay in bed desperately ill. A friend put it in his hands, and he died that same day.

Copernicus's book, along with Andreas Vesalius's *The Fabric of the Human Body* (see no. 10), also published in 1543, mark the beginning of modern science.

ANDREAS VESALIUS was born just before midnight on December 31, 1514. Both his great-grandfather and grandfather were physicians. His father was a respected apothecary to Emperor Maximilian I of the Habsburg family. Encouraged by his father to follow the family profession, Vesalius first attended the University of Louvain, near Brussels, Belgium, and then he began medical studies at the University of Paris.

Professors read from ancient books by such figures as Galen, the Greek anatomist (see no. 7), while assistants carried out sloppy dissections. Vesalius claimed he could learn more from a butcher in the meat market. In 1536, he returned to Louvain, where he seized a chance to study the human skeleton. Birds had picked clean the bones of a robber hanging on a gallows outside the city. Vesalius cut down the skeleton and studied it until he knew every bone, even while blindfolded.

On December 5, 1537, Vesalius earned his medical degree at the University of Padua, near Venice. He became professor of **anatomy** the next day. As Vesalius had promised himself, he taught anatomy by conducting **dissections** himself. Vesalius's lectures became immensely popular. Students crowded into the lecture hall to watch his skillful dissections. To show small details to the large audience, and to have something to lecture with when a cadaver was not available, Vesalius drew charts of the organs to hang in the classroom. Some of these were pirated and published without his permission. He published the rest of his charts with an anatomical manual to accompany them.

The success of the manual encouraged him to publish *The Fabric of the Human Body*. This major work was published in 1543 as seven volumes, with detailed descriptions and three hundred illustrations. Vesalius chose Jan Stephen van Calcar, a young student of the artist Titian, to refine his sketches so the essential points could be quickly grasped. The drawings showed the human body in natural poses. In his book, Vesalius detailed his own discoveries and corrected the more than two hundred errors he had found in Galen's books. He also revealed that Galen had based his anatomy theories on animal dissections.

Vesalius's book drew fierce opposition. The chief anatomist at Paris, Jacques Sylvius, attacked it as a slander against Galen. Vesalius was twenty-eight years old when he published *The Fabric of the Human Body*. After a year of defending the book, he retired from teaching and conducting anatomical research. From that point on, he served as physician in the Habsburg court—first to Emperor Charles V, grandson of Maximilian I, and then to Charles's son, Philip II, in Madrid.

At age fifty, Vesalius traveled to Jerusalem. The reason is unclear. The pilgrimage may have been taken to silence critics who accused him of impiety. Tragically, on the journey back, Vesalius died in a shipwreck off the Greek island of Zacynthus.

GALILEO GALILEI—an Italian mathematician, astronomer, and physicist—helped found the modern scientific method of deducing laws to explain the results of observation and experiment.

Galileo was born and educated in Pisa. He studied medicine at the university there but switched to mathematics. While he was still a medical student, Galileo made his first major discovery. One morning in the chapel he timed a swinging chandelier with his pulse. Experiments in his room confirmed that the time for a complete swing is the same whether the arc is a small one or a large one. The seventeen-year-old Galileo had discovered the **principle of the pendulum**, an observation overlooked by the Greeks.

Since he could not obtain a scholarship, Galileo was forced to leave the university without a degree. He earned a living as a tutor, and in 1589 was fortunate to return to the university as a professor of mathematics. When his contract at Pisa was not renewed in 1592, Galileo became professor of mathematics at the University of Padua. In an effort to understand motion, Galileo rolled balls down inclines. He established that the acceleration due to gravity acts equally on all objects regardless of their composition. He established the **law of inertia**: a body will change speed or direction only if acted upon by an outside force.

In 1609, Galileo learned of the invention of the telescope and realized its potential for scientific uses. Despite never having seen one, he deduced its construction and built one to a power of 32. He was the first to use the telescope to make astronomical observations. His instrument revealed mountains and craters on the Moon and spots on the Sun, though Aristotle had contended that the heavens were without blemish. Galileo noted that Venus has phases like the Moon, which suggested that Venus orbits the Sun. Galileo's discovery of four satellites orbiting the moving Jupiter showed that a moving Earth would not leave the Moon behind. Galileo rushed his observations into print in the book *The Sidereal Messenger* in 1610.

Galileo's fame earned him a position as court mathematician at Florence. He continued his outspoken advocacy of the Copernican view of a Sun-centered planetary system. By 1616, his critics had convinced authorities in the Catholic Church to insist that he no longer discuss the Copernican theory. He avoided the subject in public for fifteen years, but in 1632, he boldly published *Dialogue Concerning the Two Chief World Systems*, with strong arguments for the Sun-centered system.

Galileo was tried and convicted of heresy and sentenced to indefinite imprisonment, although the sentence was commuted to house arrest. Blinded by earlier damage to his eyes from looking through a telescope, Galileo was broken in body and spirit. He died in 1642 at his villa in Arcetri.

German astronomer **JOHANNES KEPLER** was a giant in his field. Born in Weil der Stadt, he studied theology at the University of Tübingen; he later turned to the field of mathematics and became a teacher in 1593. As part of his university duties, Kepler composed a yearly calendar and almanac. He used the Sun-centered planetary system because it made calculations easier.

In 1596, Kepler published *Cosmographic Mystery*. With this work, Kepler became the first well-known scientist to publicly support **Copernicus**. Kepler proposed that the Sun pushes the planets in their orbits with a force that decreases with the square of the distance. Even so, Kepler's calculations fell short of predicting celestial events to his satisfaction. He needed recent observations of the planets.

The great Danish astronomer **Tycho Brahe** (1546–1601) had extensive planetary data but had not yet prepared his observations for publication. In 1600, Kepler fled to

Prague to avoid religious persecution. He learned that Brahe had left Denmark and set up a new observatory outside Prague. Kepler became Brahe's assistant; he was to edit Brahe's data and prepare it for publication. As part of this task, Kepler tried to determine the orbit of Mars. Brahe died the next year, but Kepler continued on the problem for six years. Success came when Kepler overcame the error—held by most astronomers—that the planets traveled in combinations of circular motions.

Kepler analyzed the measurements Brahe had gathered. His analysis of the data resulted in several important discoveries. In 1609, Kepler summarized his discoveries in *The New Astronomy*. The book contained two of his **three laws of planetary motion**: (1) Planets follow paths, or orbits, that are shaped like ellipses. The Sun is at one focus of the ellipse. (2) A line connecting a planet and the Sun sweeps out equal areas in equal intervals of time. In other words, planets do not travel with uniform speed but move fastest when they are closest to the Sun.

Kepler is famous for a third astronomical law as well. The third law, which appeared in his *Harmonies of the World* (1619), says that the cube of a planet's distance from the Sun divided by the square of its period of revolution is a constant and is the same for all planets. This law means that the distance of a planet from the Sun can be calculated if its period of revolution is known.

Kepler published Brahe's data as *Rudolphine Tables* (1625). The tables remained the best ones available for several decades.

Kepler's discoveries, taken from Brahe's data, were the foundations for Isaac Newton's (see no. 20) law of universal gravitation. Kepler died in 1630 in Regensburg, Bavaria.

◆ **WILLIAM HARVEY** came from an English family wealthy enough to send him to the University of Cambridge. After earning a bachelor's degree, he began medical studies at the University of Padua in Italy. Harvey embraced the concept of **experimental science** and applied it to medical subjects. He studied under **Hieronymus Fabricius**, who had discovered one-way valves in the veins.

During this time, anatomy was used to explain the structure of the body; however, understanding the functions of the organs lagged behind. Doctors believed veins carried blood in a slow and irregular flow away from the heart. The Greek physician **Galen** (see no. 7) taught that the liver manufactured new blood to replace the old. It was thought that the beat of the heart was caused by a surge of blood through it.

In 1602 William Harvey earned his medical degree and returned to England. He married well and began a successful practice with medical research in London. He compared the tissues of the heart with muscles and saw that the heart was a strong bundle of muscles. The structure of the heart was so similar to the parts of a water pump that he concluded the heart was a blood pump. He calculated that in one hour the heart pumped seven gallons of blood, far more than the liver could deliver. Blood had to circulate in a closed path so it could be reused. His experiments showed that veins carried blood to the heart. He realized that the little valves that Fabricius discovered kept blood from flowing backward.

In 1616, Harvey presented his first lecture on the **circulation of blood** to London's Royal College of Physicians. He published his views in 1628. *On the Motion of the Heart and Blood in Animals* ran to only fifty-two printed pages, but it established his case with an overwhelming mound of evidence. The book generated intense interest and resulted in heated discussions between his supporters and opponents. Critics called him Circulator to put him in the company of medical frauds who went from village to village (circulating), selling phony medical remedies. The only true criticism they could raise was that he had failed to demonstrate how the blood was conveyed from the arteries to the veins.

Most of Harvey's other writings, such as an autopsy of a man reputed to be 152 years old, were ordinary. However, Harvey lived to be eighty years old, long enough to see his groundbreaking work fully accepted. Four years after he died in London, Marcello Malpighi (1628–1694) detected the tiny capillaries connecting arteries to veins. Harvey had predicted their existence.

RENÉ DESCARTES

1596–1650

RENÉ DESCARTES was one of the most influential philosophers and mathematicians in history. Descartes was born in La Haye, France, the son of a minor nobleman who was not especially wealthy. At age eight, Descartes began studies at the college of La Flèche, a Jesuit boarding school. After five years of a classical education, he received three years of instruction in mathematics and new scientific ideas. One of these new scientific beliefs was a great respect for experimentation. The contrast of the experimental method to his previous classical learning caused Descartes to doubt what he had been taught. This skepticism was the foundation for his later philosophy.

Wishing to travel, Descartes joined the army of Prince Maurice of the Netherlands in 1616. Later, he traveled in summers and spent winters in towns of his liking. In 1629, he relocated to Holland because of its climate of intellectual freedom.

In Holland, Descartes began first book, *Rules for the Direction of the Mind* (1629), which was not published during his lifetime.

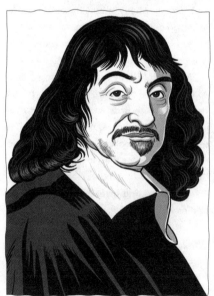

He began a second book, *The World* (1633), but halted work when he learned the Catholic Church opposed Copernicus. A third book, *Discourse on Method* (1637), was published with great impact. It established Descartes as a major force in modern philosophy. In this work, he discussed the nature of knowledge and the process of learning new information. His famous phrase "I think, therefore I am" was used to demonstrate the existence of the self as well as God. Descartes included three long articles about his scientific studies at the back of *Discourse on Method*. One study detailed the **fundamental law of reflection**, which Descartes discovered: the angle an incoming ray makes with the perpendicular to a reflecting surface is equal to the angle the reflected ray makes to the perpendicular.

The third appendix in *Discourse on Method* was of vast importance to scientists because it described Descartes's invention of analytical (coordinate) geometry. Analytical geometry combined algebra and geometry. Geometric figures were studied by placing them on x and y coordinate axes. With this system, any point on a geometric figure can be located by giving its distance from the x- and y-axes.

This allows geometric figures to be described in a numerical way. Descartes also invented the idea of using letters at the end of the alphabet for unknowns and superscripts to represent powers.

In 1649, the twenty-three-year-old **Queen Christina of Sweden** invited Descartes to her court as her private tutor. After he arrived, he learned that she had scheduled the classes at five o'clock in the morning. Unfortunately, Descartes did not survive the first Stockholm winter. Four months after moving to Sweden he died of pneumonia.

BLAISE PASCAL grew up in wealthy circumstances. His father was a rich merchant and a member of the nobility. After Pascal's mother died when he was three, his father saw to his son's education and hired tutors to teach him at home. Pascal's father decided to lock away books about geometry until Pascal was fifteen years old to focus his son's attention on other studies. However, at age twelve Pascal began using his playtime to secretly study geometry.

In 1630, the family moved to Paris, and Pascal impressed scientific gatherings with his own studies of conic sections. In 1639, Pascal's father was appointed tax collector for Upper Normandy. To aid in his father's mission, Pascal built a mechanical calculator, the first of its kind, when he was nineteen years old.

Pascal was a firm believer in conducting experiments rather than using reasoning alone. His experiments showed that a liquid rises in a barometer because of air pressure rather than the pull of a vacuum at the top of the tube. By 1648 he had established **Pascal's principle**: a fluid in a container transmits pressure equally in all directions and acts at right angles to the surfaces it contacts.

Along with French lawyer and mathematician **Pierre de Fermat** (1601–1665), Pascal developed the laws of probability. Pascal and de Fermat's results have applications from insurance mortality tables to the decay of subatomic particles. **Pascal's triangle**, a deceptively simple arrangement of numbers in which each number is the sum of the two numbers immediately above it, provides the coefficients of the binomial expansion, combinations used in probability, and other number series.

Throughout his life, Pascal had been interested in pursuing a better understanding of the Christian faith. At the age of thirty-two, he had a frightening accident. While he was riding in a carriage, the horses bolted and the carriage was left hanging over a bridge. Pascal was rescued, but the accident changed the direction of his life. From that point on, he devoted himself almost completely to religious matters. His writings are noted for their logic and passion. The sparkle of his *Provincial Letters* (1656) marked the beginning of the era of modern French prose.

Pascal's most famous philosophic work is *Pensées*, a collection of personal thoughts on human suffering and faith, written about 1658. He could write with authority about pain because he constantly suffered migraine headaches and stomach ulcers. *Pensées* was never finished, and the correct way to compose the notes he left behind has fueled philosophical discussions to this day.

Pascal died at the age of thirty-nine, probably from a malignant ulcer of the stomach. Despite his short life, he left his mark in a variety of fields including physics, mathematics, geometry, philosophy, and Christian literature.

Of English heritage, **ROBERT BOYLE** was born at Lismore Castle, in Ireland. He was the seventh son of the Great Earl of Cork, one of the richest men in the world. To ensure that his sons did not become pampered and spoiled, the Great Earl sent them to be raised by poor families. From the age of six months to four years, Robert Boyle lived in the home of an Irish peasant family. He was educated by tutors until he turned eight, and then he studied in England at Eton for three years.

By the time he was twenty, Boyle had moved to London and become associated with a group of experimental scientists. Boyle strongly believed the future of science lay with the experimental method. His motto, "nothing by mere authority," rejected the idea that ancient books had all of the answers. His group held informal talks in one another's homes, and Boyle gave it the name "the invisible college."

In 1654, Boyle moved to Oxford, to be closer to the proponents of experimental science. With the assistance of the brilliant **Robert Hooke** (see no. 19), he built an improved air pump.

Together they proved that sound does not travel in a vacuum. They confirmed Galileo's contention that, without air resistance, a feather and a lump of lead fall at the same speed. Boyle admitted he had been unable to fully pursue his study of respiration in a vacuum because he could not bring himself to cause suffering to animals.

Boyle published these findings in *Touching the Spring of the Air* (1660). The book contained Boyle's law that the volume of a gas varies inversely to its pressure.

Boyle's greatest achievements were in chemistry. He defined an element as a substance that cannot be chemically reduced to other simpler substances and cannot be produced by combining two or more simpler substances.

His book *The Sceptical Chemist* (1661) marked the **beginning of modern chemistry**.

Boyle urged his fellow scientists to report their experiments quickly so others might know of new discoveries. In 1663, he led the successful effort to charter the **Royal Society** as a formal scientific body patterned after the "invisible college." In 1668, he returned to London and built a chemical laboratory in his home. He discovered the flammable element **phosphorus** and created the first match.

Besides his scientific investigations, Robert Boyle learned Hebrew, Greek, and Syriac to pursue his study of Scripture. He was offered but turned down a variety of posts, including provost of Eton, a position in the Church of England, and president of the Royal Society. Boyle never married. When he died in London, his will left his scientific collection and equipment to the Royal Society and provided for a yearly lecture for "proving the Christian religion against the attack of infidels."

CHRISTIAAN HUYGENS was born in The Hague, Netherlands, to a family that greatly valued learning and scientific study. He received a good education that included instruction at home from his father, private tutors, and attendance at the University of Leiden. Huygens became interested in telescopes while helping his brother construct one. Telescopes of Huygens's era produced poor images because the lens acted as a prism and formed a different image for each color. Huygens's solution was to employ a lens of long focal length. He built a telescope with a main lens two inches in diameter, but with a focal length of twenty-three feet. Making and using such a cumbersome telescope took skill and patience.

In 1656, Huygens discovered the **Orion Nebula** and detected stars embedded in it. His telescope revealed surface markings on Mars. Huygens was the first to draw the distinctive V-shaped feature known as Syrtis Major. He discovered a large satellite of Saturn, which he named **Titan**. In Galileo's telescope, Saturn appeared to have two handles. Huygens saw that the handles were really a ring that encircled the planet.

To time astronomical events, Huygens built a clock capable of keeping time to the minute. He used the regular back-and-forth motion of a swinging pendulum to control the gears and a series of slowly falling weights on a chain to keep the pendulum in motion. He presented the first working model to the Dutch government and described it in printed form in 1658. The pendulum clock became known as the grandfather clock.

In 1663, Huygens visited London, where the Royal Society elected him a member. Three years later, **King Louis XIV** invited Huygens to France and requested that he start a French organization patterned after the English Royal Society. In 1668, the French **Royal Academy of Science** began meeting with Huygens as the first president. Huygens published his most important work, *Horologium Oscillatorium* (1673), in this period. In the book he described the physics of pendulum motion. He also described the formula for centripetal force in circular motion, which aided Isaac Newton (see no. 20) in calculating the force of gravity acting between the Earth and Moon.

In 1681 intolerance toward Protestants in Paris caused Huygens to return to the Netherlands. He refined his wave theory of light, the chief rival to Newton's particle theory of light. Huygens had discovered the polarization of light. He interpreted polarization, reflection, and refraction, using his wave theory. A book about light he had begun years earlier, *Traité de la Lumière*, was published in 1678. It contains **Huygens's principle**: every point on a wave acts as a new source of waves.

ANTONIE VAN LEEUWENHOEK, a pioneer of **microscopic research**, was born in Delft, Holland. He left school at sixteen to be an apprentice in a dry-goods store in Amsterdam. At the age of twenty-one, he returned to Delft to open a drapery store. Leeuwenhoek began to use simple magnifying glasses to examine the quality of cloth. As a hobby, he built microscopes and observed objects through them. The lens for Leeuwenhoek's most powerful microscope was no bigger than the head of a pin, but it magnified things 270 times.

The lens was attached to a brass holder, and he mounted the specimen to be examined on a bolt attached to the lens holder. By turning the bolt, the object could be brought into fine focus.

Leeuwenhoek possessed a never-ending curiosity. He examined hair, skin, cork, ivory, blood, the eyes and wings of insects, and muscle tissue through his microscopes. He observed that red blood cells in arteries

squeezed through capillaries and came out on the other side in veins. He was also the first to observe sperm cells. He carefully recorded what he saw and made detailed drawings.

Beginning in 1673, he started sending letters to the Royal Society in London. Rather than writing in Latin, the language of scholars, Leeuwenhoek wrote in Dutch. His letters were informal and chatty, as if he were addressing a friend rather than a gathering of the world's greatest scientists. Despite their amusement at his style, members of the Royal Society asked him for additional reports.

Leeuwenhoek made hundreds of microscopes so he could keep specimens permanently mounted for later study. Because of his experience and patience, he saw details that other scientists entirely missed. His study of the life cycles of small insects such as fleas and ants convinced him that they arose in the same way as larger animals, and not by spontaneous generation.

In 1674, Leeuwenhoek found single-celled animals, **protozoa**, growing in water from stagnant ponds. He calculated that a single drop of water would be home to one million of the little animals. This report aroused skepticism at the Royal Society, but he succeeded in countering it by sending twenty of his microscopes. In 1680, the Royal Society elected him a member. Three years later they published one of his drawings of bacteria.

Leeuwenhoek enjoyed good health, a long life, and considerable honors. His fame was so widespread that he was visited by several reigning monarchs, including King Frederick I of Prussia and Czar Peter the Great of Russia. By the time of his death, at the age of ninety, Leeuwenhoek had made more than four hundred microscopes.

ROBERT HOOKE was born on the Isle of Wight. An orphan at the age of thirteen, he was frail and undersized as a child. As a young man, he earned a living by waiting tables and used the money to attend the University of Oxford. In 1655, while at Oxford, Hooke became the physicist **Robert Boyle's** (see no. 16) assistant. With the improved air pump they built, he and Boyle proved that both combustion and respiration required air, and that sound would not travel in a vacuum.

Shortly before it was officially chartered in 1663, the Royal Society employed Hooke as curator of experiments, a position he filled until his death. He demonstrated interesting new ideas to the members each week and performed thousands of experiments over the next forty years.

While studying a thin slice of cork with an improved microscope of his design, Hooke observed a regular pattern of honeycomb-like pores. He called them **cells**. His finding was the first clue that cells are the building blocks of life. In 1665 Hooke published his book *Micrographia*. The book contains some of the most beautiful drawings of tiny subjects ever made: snowflakes, feathers, fish scales, and living organisms such as molds and mosses. His portrait of a flea is a classic that is often reproduced. He recognized that fossils were remains of past life.

Following London's Great Fire of 1666, he worked with architect Christopher Wren to help rebuild the city. Hooke held the office of surveyor of London and designed some of the buildings, including Bethlehem Hospital.

After one of the meetings of the Royal Society, Hooke, Wren, and astronomer **Edmund Halley** met and discussed the nature of gravity. Hooke stated that gravity grows weaker by the square of the distance. He never succeeded in proving the idea correct. Halley then took the problem to **Sir Isaac Newton** (see no. 20), who supplied the proof. In Newton's masterpiece, *Principia*, he acknowledged Hooke's contribution.

Hooke invented a large number of **weather instruments**, including an improved barometer and a device to measure humidity. He developed the balance spring to regulate watches, which made small, but accurate, timekeepers possible. Though Hooke made great contributions to science, his life seems to have been neither easy nor happy. He seldom finished many of the projects he undertook. In addition, he had the misfortune to live at the same time as Newton and never succeeded in emerging from the shadow of that great intellect.

Today, Hooke is most remembered for his **law of elasticity** (1678). That law states that the amount a solid is deformed is directly proportional to the force acting on it. Spring scales for weighing produce in supermarkets use this principle.

ISAAC NEWTON was born on Christmas Day on a farm at Woolsthorpe, England. His father had died before his birth. Newton was an ordinary student, although he did exhibit some talent—he carved intricate models of objects, such as a gristmill that actually worked. In 1661, after Newton proved to be inept as a farmer, his uncle suggested he attend Trinity College, Cambridge; during his time there he gained no particular notice.

In 1665, Cambridge was dismissed because of the plague. During the forced leave, Newton developed a simple rule for calculating the terms of a binomial expression raised to any power. He also studied light. His experiments with prisms proved that white light contains all colors of the spectrum. In addition, Newton conducted studies in gravity—which are among the most famous and important scientific studies of all time. After observing an apple fall, Newton realized that the force of gravity acting on it was the force that acted on the Moon to hold it in orbit around the Earth. The

law of universal gravitation was revealed—objects experience a gravitational force proportional to the inverse square of the distance separating them and proportional to the product of their masses.

Newton returned to Cambridge in 1667. In three years, he received an appointment as professor of mathematics. Newton built a reflecting telescope, the first of its kind. A mirror, unlike a lens, acts on all colors in the same way. The instrument had a one-inch mirror and was about six inches long. It compared favorably to a lens telescope several feet long. A gift of an improved telescope to the Royal Society resulted in Newton's being elected to that body.

Newton developed calculus, a powerful mathematical tool, but did not publish his findings. When Gottfried Wilhelm Leibniz published his own version of calculus in 1684, Newton's English friends fought a battle to ensure that Newton received credit. Newton himself avoided the controversy.

Newton was so immersed in his studies that he did not want to take time to write and publish his findings. The astronomer Edmund Halley finally persuaded Newton to publish his work. As a result, Newton's most important findings were published in *Principia Mathematica* in 1687. He stated his **three laws of motion** and the law of universal gravitation.

Newton's greatest achievement was to demonstrate that scientific principles are of universal application. He clearly defined the nature of mass, weight, force, inertia, and acceleration.

Newton was elected president of the Royal Society in 1703 and served until his death. In 1707, Queen Anne knighted him, the first scientist so honored. He was buried in Westminster Abbey, beside England's historical leaders.

Known for his studies of the stars, **EDMUND HALLEY** was born in London, England. He studied at Oxford but left without a degree to become an astronomer. One of his first astronomical projects was to chart star positions in the southern skies from the island of St. Helena in the south Atlantic. One of the stars that he examined, **Omega Centauri**, turned out to be a globular cluster—the first one ever discovered. It was a swarm of 300,000 stars.

Halley also investigated the Large and Small **Magellanic Clouds**, which appeared as detached parts of the Milky Way. After observing a transit of Mercury across the face of the Sun, he proposed using transits of the inner planets to measure the distance of the Sun. Halley's two-year stay at St. Helena, from 1676 to 1678, gave him a precisely plotted framework of 341 southern stars. Upon his return to London, he published his star catalog. The Royal Society elected him a member at the age of twenty-two, and Oxford granted him a master's degree.

In 1686, Halley, scientist Robert Hooke, and architect Christopher Wren met and discussed the subject of gravity. Wren challenged the scientists to show that the planets would travel in elliptical orbits given the assumption that gravity decreased by the square of the distance. Both Hooke and Halley failed to supply the proof. Halley took the problem to mathematician Isaac Newton at Cambridge. During their conversation, Halley realized that Newton had many unpublicized discoveries. Halley urged Newton to publish his findings and promised to take care of the many details of seeing a book through to publication. In the next eighteen months, Newton wrote *Principia Mathematica*, which established his reputation. Halley paid for its publication with his own funds.

In 1693, Halley prepared statistical mortality tables, the first of their kind. In 1698, he went to sea for three years, as commander of a British naval vessel that measured magnetic variations. For years he had collected information about comets. In 1703, he began calculating their orbits. He found that those of 1531, 1607, and 1682 had orbits so similar they must be the same comet. In 1705, he predicted the return of this comet in 1758; it is known today as **Halley's comet.**

Halley learned Arabic to translate ancient Greek manuscripts that existed only in that language. In 1718, he reviewed Greek star maps and found that in 1,500 years **Sirius**, the brightest star in the sky, had moved about the width of the full moon. Halley announced that stars had a proper motion and were not truly fixed.

In 1720, Halley succeeded John Flamsteed as Astronomer Royal. Halley died in 1742 in Greenwich, England, at the age of eighty-six.

DANIEL BERNOULLI was born in the Netherlands, but his family moved to Switzerland when he was five years old. Both Bernoulli's father, Johann, and his uncle, Jackob, were noted mathematicians, and the next generation of Bernoullis followed in their footsteps.

Daniel's older brother studied law, but became a mathematician in St. Petersburg, in Russia. Daniel's younger brother became a professor of language but took over the mathematics chair at the University of Basel, Switzerland, upon the death of his father. By the age of twenty-one, Daniel Bernoulli had become a physician. As part of his thesis for a doctorate, he applied mathematics to the action of the lungs. A scientific researcher at heart, Daniel Bernoulli never practiced medicine.

In 1726, the Russian Academy invited Bernoulli to teach mathematics. From that post, his scientific research continued.

Bernoulli became the first European of note to accept Newtonian physics. Newton's laws had been applied to larger objects such as the Moon and planets. Bernoulli applied

the laws to smaller particles, including those that made up fluids such as gases and liquids. In 1728, he brought his mathematical skill to bear on the problem of gas laws. He assumed that gases contained particles with sizes that were small compared to the distances separating them.

Applying the laws of probability to the invisible atoms, he provided a secondary proof of **Boyle's law**: the pressure of a gas is inversely related to its volume.

After seven years in Russia, Bernoulli returned to the University of Basel, where he held positions as professor of botany, then anatomy, and finally physics. In 1738, he published *Hydrodynamica*, dealing with the motions of fluids. Daniel Bernoulli was one of the first scientists to understand the concept of **conservation of energy**. The motion of a fluid gave it kinetic energy and the pressure of the fluid gave it potential energy. A fluid that increased speed had to lose pressure to keep the total energy constant. *Hydrodynamica* contains his most important result, **Bernoulli's principle**: as the speed of a moving fluid increases, the pressure within the fluid decreases. Bernoulli's principle applies to both liquids and gases.

Bernoulli's studies of fluid flow had many practical applications. For example, Bernoulli distinguished between laminar flow and turbulent flow. He showed that fluids that flowed in layers did so more smoothly and required less energy than turbulent flow.

Therefore, ships with a shape that promoted laminar flow passed through water more efficiently than those that created eddies and wakes.

Bernoulli and his family made a significant impact on science and mathematics. At least five laws, principles, and equations bear the Bernoulli name.

BENJAMIN FRANKLIN'S impressive career included work as a publisher, author, inventor, scientist, and diplomat. He was the first scientist of note in the American colonies. Franklin was the fifteenth of seventeen children born to a poor candle maker. He attended only two years of grammar school. He worked first for his father and then for his brother, a printer. In 1723, at the age of seventeen, he struck out on his own.

The next year, a Philadelphia store owner sent him to England as a buyer. Problems with the letters of credit left him stranded in London. He lived in England for eighteen months before he found passage back to the colonies. In Philadelphia, he opened his own print shop. He started a newspaper and printed *Poor Richard's Almanack*.

Turning his interests to science, in 1743, Franklin established that the prevailing storm track in North America was from the southwest. His study of heat led him to build a cast-iron stove that sat out in a room and was more efficient at heating than a fireplace. He described the **Franklin stove** in a pamphlet in 1744 but did not patent it. The Franklin stove later became a common fixture in the colonies and in Europe.

Franklin's electrical experiments began in 1747 when he acquired a Leyden jar, an early form of the capacitor, a device that stores electric charge. He used plus (+) and minus (–) to represent an excess or deficit of electricity. He established **three laws of static electricity**: (1) unlike electrical charges attract, (2) like electrical charges repel, and (3) a charged body will attract an uncharged nonconductor. Franklin sent letters about his experiment to friends in England, who read them before the Royal Society. In 1751, his discoveries were printed in an eighty-page pamphlet. Franklin became famous throughout Europe as a scientist and was elected a member of the Society.

In 1752, Franklin proved that lightning is a static discharge by conducting his famous spectacular and dangerous kite-flying experiment during a thunderstorm. Lightning that he captured in a Leyden jar had the same properties as static electricity. Franklin observed that static electricity dissipated when a sharply pointed conductor was brought nearby. He invented lightning rods to protect wooden buildings against fires started by lightning bolts.

From 1757 to 1775 Franklin represented the interests of the colonies in England. During this time, he invented bifocal glasses and publicized the existence of the Gulf Stream. As British rule grew more oppressive, he saw independence from England as the only solution. In 1776, he helped draft the **Declaration of Independence** and was one of its signatories. He represented the United States in France during the Revolutionary War. Franklin was equal parts great statesman and great scientist.

LEONHARD EULER was born in Basel, Switzerland, and attended the university there with the intention of becoming a minister, like his father. However, science and mathematics held more interest for him than Hebrew and theology. Professor Johann Bernoulli, one of his father's friends, interceded to allow Euler to major in mathematics.

After Euler graduated, Empress **Catherine I** of Russia invited him to St. Petersburg as a teacher of applied mathematics. After serving as a medical officer in the Russian navy for three years, Euler became a full professor of physics. In 1733, he took the mathematics post vacated by Daniel Bernoulli, Johann's son. With the increased salary, Euler married Katharina Gsell. They had thirteen children, although only five survived their infancy. Euler's powers of concentration were legendary. He claimed he did some of his best work while his children played at his feet.

In 1736, Euler wrote *Mechanica*, which

recast Newtonian physics, changing geometric proofs to modern analytical methods. He wrote equations to predict the flow, turbulence, and pressure exerted by fluids. The science of air flight makes use of Euler's equations.

When Russian politics became unstable, Euler moved to Germany, at the urging of Prussian King Frederick the Great. At the Berlin Academy, Euler applied mathematics to subjects such as planetary orbits, ballistics, shipbuilding, navigation, optics, and acoustics. He also improved **mathematical nomenclature** (a set of names and terms). He introduced the Greek letter *sigma*, for sum; *pi* for the ratio of the circumference of a circle to its radius; *e* as the base of the natural logarithms; *i* to stand for the square root of –1 (imaginary numbers); and *f(x)* for a function.

Eventually Euler grew tired of Frederick's interference in the Berlin Academy. After twenty-five years at Berlin, Euler returned to St. Petersburg and remained there until his death. In the last years of his life, Euler became totally blind. However, because of his exceptional memory, and the help of his son, Johann, this handicap did not diminish his output. He wrote a three-volume book, *Letters to a Princess of Germany* (1768–1772), to explain the main concepts of science. Euler tackled the three-body problem to calculate the Moon's orbit under the gravitational influence of Earth and Sun. **Lunar motion** was important to captains of sailing ships for calculating longitude. His treatment was the best available method for more than a hundred years.

In all, during his lifetime, Euler produced more than eight hundred papers. After his death, St. Petersburg Academy continued to print Euler's previously unpublished works for nearly fifty more years.

CAROLUS LINNAEUS was born in a turf-roofed farmhouse in a rural area of Råshut, Sweden, where his father was a pastor. By the age of eight, Linneaus had earned the nickname the "little botanist" because of his interest in plants. He chose medicine as his career because doctors prescribed herbs and extracted drugs from plants. He found the herb garden at the University of Lund insufficient, so he transferred to the University of Uppsala near Stockholm. Uppsala had better botanical gardens and more books on the subject. Linnaeus worked with **Olaf Celsius**, a professor of religious studies who was an experienced naturalist and an authority on plants that were mentioned in the Bible.

In 1730, Linnaeus gave lectures on **botany** at Uppsala although he had not yet graduated. Letters from students about the plants they saw on their travels made him eager to undertake field studies. In 1732, Linnaeus trekked 4,600 miles through Lapland gathering flora. The next year he moved to Holland, where he received a medical degree. In 1735, he published *Systema Naturae* to describe his classification of the hundreds of plants he had discovered. The book began as seven large pages and eventually grew to 2,500 pages in later editions.

After visits to London and Paris, Linnaeus settled in Stockholm in 1738 and began a medical practice. He successfully treated members of the Queen's court and was appointed physician to the Admiralty. After his marriage to the daughter of a physician, he returned to Uppsala as professor of medicine in 1741. Then he and a fellow professor switched roles so Linnaeus could chair the biology department. In 1751, Linnaeus published *Philosophia Botanica*, his most important book. In it, Linnaeus fully developed the **binomial nomenclature** (a naming system in biology). He gave a specific name to each plant and collected similar species into larger groups, or genuses. The two labels, genus and species, made the name for each plant. He applied his binomial naming convention to animals, including humans (*Homo sapiens*). In this way, he provided an organized scheme for naming plants and animals.

In all, Linnaeus wrote about 180 works during his lifetime. In 1761, he was appointed to the Swedish House of Nobles. He continued to teach and inspire his students. In 1772, he suffered a stroke, which weakened him. After his death six years later, his widow sold his collections of specimens and books to a wealthy English naturalist, Sir James Edward Smith. In 1788, the material became part of the newly created **Linnaean Society**, the first organization devoted exclusively to naturalist studies.

HENRY CAVENDISH came from an aristocratic English family. Sadly, his mother died when he was two years old. He developed into a profoundly shy individual. Although he received an excellent education at Cambridge, he chose not to graduate rather than face the professors at his final examination. Over the years, his shyness grew more intense. Except for occasional meetings of the Royal Society, he could not face more than one man at a time, and women not at all. He never married. Female servants were ordered to avoid him. As he walked through his mansion, they scurried out of his sight. He communicated with them by leaving notes.

Cavendish experimented with gases and was the first to measure their densities. He discovered **hydrogen** when he released the gas by treating metals with muriatic (hydrochloric) acid. He showed that it was the lightest of all gases and that hydrogen's reaction with oxygen produced water.

In the 1770s, he brought electricity to

bear on his study of gases. Cavendish measured the strength of electricity by grasping an electrode and noting how far up his arm the muscles twitched! During an experiment with nitrogen, he detected argon, an inert gas. He sent an electric spark through a sample of air to combine the nitrogen with oxygen. A small bubble of the more-inert argon gas remained uncombined.

In 1798, Cavendish succeeded in measuring the tiny gravitational force acting between bodies of ordinary size. He suspended a bar with weights on each end from a fine wire. The attraction of larger balls to the smaller ones caused the wire to twist slightly. With the room sealed to avoid stray air currents, he peered through a window with a telescope. A mirror on the wire reflected a beam of light and amplified the slight twisting motion. Measuring the force of gravity for objects of known mass allowed Cavendish to calculate the mass of the Earth, using the universal law of gravitation.

Cavendish was one of the wealthiest—and most eccentric—men of science. He made extravagant expenditures for scientific apparatus and books. He moved his large library to London so other scientists could use it but would not bother him when borrowing books. He dressed in clothes long out of style. The only portrait of him was made without his knowledge.

Cavendish carried out scientific experiments simply because he enjoyed doing so. Although he took careful notes, he published only twenty short papers. Cavendish enjoyed good health all of his life, and the only illness he suffered caused his death at the age of seventy-eight. In the 1860s, physicist **James Clerk Maxwell** reviewed Cavendish's papers and published them. The **Cavendish Laboratory** is named in his honor.

Englishman **JOSEPH PRIESTLEY** combined the fields of **religion and science**. Born in Leeds, in northern England, he received early training from a local Calvinist minister and from an academy of **Dissenters**. (Dissenters were those people who opposed the Church of England.) Priestley's first job was as assistant minister to an independent Presbyterian congregation. In 1758, he operated a day school where he demonstrated recent scientific experiments for the students. He published the *Rudiments of English Grammar* (1761), a textbook that remained in use for fifty years.

The following year was an eventful one. He was ordained a minister, married eighteen-year-old Mary Wilkinson, and met the American statesman Benjamin Franklin in London. Franklin encouraged him to experiment with electricity. He enthusiastically did so, despite a lack of scientific training. Priestley had an early success when he showed that carbon, a nonmetal, would conduct electricity. This discovery and his book, *History and Present State of Electricity* (1767), gained him admission to England's Royal Society.

In 1767, two of Priestley's lifelong interests continued to converge. He became pastor at a chapel near his hometown of Leeds and continued his scientific research. He studied the gas given off by fermentation from a brewery next to his home. The gas was heavier than air and would smother flames. He dissolved it in water to produce the first carbonated beverage. Priestley had discovered **carbon dioxide.**

Chemists caught gases by leading them through a tube to a beaker full of water that was held upside down in a water bath. As the gas bubbled out of the tube, it filled the beaker and drove out the water. The procedure failed if gases dissolved in water.

Priestley substituted mercury for water and captured a variety of new gases, including carbon monoxide, nitrous oxide (laughing gas), and ammonia.

In 1772, the Earl of Shelburne employed him as his personal librarian. In this position, Priestley had more time for research. In 1774, he received a powerful burning glass. With this he focused the rays of the Sun on a compound of mercury in a closed test tube. The heated compound released a gas. When he thrust a glowing ember into the gas, it burst into flame. Mice placed in a container of the gas became very active. Priestley had discovered oxygen.

Priestley had become a Unitarian with unpopular religious views, and he began expressing his religious and political views more forcibly. In 1791, a mob burned down his home, library, and laboratory. He managed to escape with his family to London. His three sons emigrated to the United States; Priestley and his wife joined them in 1794.

WILLIAM HERSCHEL was born in Hanover, Germany, during the time it was ruled by King George II of England. When Herschel was nineteen years old, the Seven Years War spilled into Hanover, and he escaped to England. He changed his given name of Wilhelm to William and worked as a musician and composer while he taught himself mathematics and astronomy. In 1766, he became organist in the resort town of Bath; his sister Caroline, who had come to join him, sang in the choir.

Herschel taught himself Latin and Italian so he could read books about music. One of the books used mathematics to explain the harmonics of organ pipes. After studying books on astronomy, he began making his own telescopes. By 1774, his telescopes rivaled those in the best observatories. Herschel made mirror telescopes because of their simple design and light-gathering power.

On March 13, 1781, during one of his surveys of the sky, he saw a faint disk of light

of magnitude 6. It was barely visible to the unaided eyes. He had discovered **Uranus,** a planet even farther from the Sun than Saturn. Later Herschel detected two moons of the planet. He named them **Titania** and **Oberon**, names taken from Shakespeare's *A Midsummer Night's Dream*; this was a break from the custom of astronomers using Greek mythology as a source for names.

In 1782, he and Caroline gave their last public musical performances. That year he became a professional astronomer when he became the court astronomer to King George III. In 1788, Herschel married Mary Pitt, a wealthy widow who lived next door. The following year he built a 48-inch telescope, the largest in the world. With his wife to manage the house, and Caroline to record his observations, he entered a period of unparalleled productivity.

Over the next twenty years, Herschel identified 2,500 nebulae and star clusters. At first, he believed that with a powerful enough telescope, all nebulae could be resolved into individual stars. He believed the more distant ones to be island universes (galaxies) similar to the **Milky Way**. Later, he realized some of the nebulae were clouds of gas illuminated by embedded stars. He found 848 double stars. Most of them orbited each other and proved that the law of gravity extended beyond the solar system. In 1800, he detected invisible infrared light while experimenting with a thermometer and the Sun's spectrum.

Herschel's discoveries revitalized science. His son **John Herschel** extended his observations to southern skies. His sister Caroline returned to Hanover and lived to the age of ninety-eight. She was recognized as the first professional female astronomer.

ANTOINE-LAURENT LAVOISIER was born in Paris, the son of lawyer. His education included the study of the classics, mathematics, and sciences. Following in his father's footsteps, Lavoisier received his law degree in 1764. However, an interest in rocks and minerals led him into a study of chemistry.

Lavoisier is noted for making measurements an essential part of chemistry. For example, he borrowed a precision balance from the French mint and used it to test the belief of chemists that boiling water produces a solid residue. Lavoisier boiled distilled water in a closed glass container for 101 days.

Flakes of sand-like material formed. Yet, the weight of the water after boiling was the same as before. The glass container had lost weight equal to the weight of the flakes. Lavoisier showed that hot water had dissolved some of the glass and deposited it as solid residue.

Later he burned a diamond in a closed container. It combined with oxygen to produce carbon dioxide. Despite changing from a solid to a gas, Lavoisier showed that there was no change in weight. Lavoisier stated the **law of conservation of mass**: mass can neither be created nor destroyed during chemical change. Lavoisier also demonstrated that burning is a process of oxidation. He destroyed the incorrect theory that a substance called phlogiston was released during combustion.

In 1771, Lavoisier married Marie Anne Paulze, who assisted him in his work. She took notes, drew illustrations, and translated his work into English. Lavoisier invested money with his wife's father, who ran a company that collected taxes for the government. Lavoisier held a variety of public offices, such as director of the gunpowder administration. He served on a committee on agriculture and started a model farm. In 1790, he became a member of the commission on weights and measures that moved the country toward use of the **metric system.**

Lavoisier's *Method of Chemical Nomenclature* (1787) established an organized system for naming chemical compounds. His system gave compounds names that reflected their composition. For example, "fixed air" was named carbon dioxide because it contained carbon and oxygen. In his *Treatise on Chemical Elements* (1789), Lavoisier listed the new gases oxygen, nitrogen, and hydrogen as elements, and showed that water was a compound of oxygen and hydrogen. He identified thirty-three chemical elements.

In 1793, during the **French Revolution**, the fate of the country fell into the hands of the Committee of Public Safety. As a despised tax collector, Lavoisier was arrested. On May 8, 1794, he was tried, convicted, and sentenced to death. On that same day, he was taken to the guillotine. Lavoisier's body was tossed in a common grave. Ironically, within two years, the French were building statues honoring him.

◆ **ALESSANDRO VOLTA** was born in Como, northern Italy. He was one of nine children of a noble family that had fallen into poor circumstances. The young boy did so poorly in grammar school that his parents feared he might be mentally handicapped. However, by his early teens, his mental gifts had become apparent. At age fourteen, his educational performance had improved enough that he began to pursue a career in science.

Volta became professor of physics at the Royal School of Como in 1774. The next year, he invented the **electrophorus**, a device capable of both generating and storing static electricity. It had an insulated hard rubber pad on the bottom and a metal plate with a handle on top. The hard rubber took on a negative charge when rubbed. By grounding the upper plate and repeating the process, a strong separation of charge accumulated between the two plates.

One year later Volta was appointed to the chair of physics at the University of Pavia. While he served in this position, Volta's friend, **Luigi Galvani**, reported some puzzling observations to him in 1780. Galvani, a medical scientist, noticed that the leg of a dead frog jumped when he touched it with an object that had a static electric charge. He wondered if lightning would also cause a dead frog's leg to twitch. He placed the legs on brass hooks. When a thunderstorm passed nearby, the frog legs moved.

Volta conducted his own experiments in 1794 to find out more about how electricity is generated. When Volta touched the legs of a dead frog with two different metals, such as copper and zinc, the legs jumped. Volta also found that animal tissue was not needed to produce a current. He replaced the frog legs with a piece of cloth soaked in salt then attached two metal samples to the cloth. He found that two different metals separated by salt water produced electricity. He applied this discovery by creating the **voltaic cell**. His cell consisted of a copper disk separated from a zinc disk by a fabric disk soaked in salt water. When Volta touched the top and bottom metal disks with a wire, a faint electric current flowed through it. A chemical reaction produced an electric current.

To increase the amount of electricity, Volta stacked several voltaic cells together. By 1800, Alessandro Volta developed the **first electric battery**. It produced a steady stream of electricity by chemical action. In 1801 in Paris, he demonstrated his battery to Napoleon, who made Volta a count. Volta's discoveries enlarged the science of electricity to include current electricity as well as static electricity. The volt, the unit of electrical potential, is named in his honor.

EDWARD JENNER grew up in the village of Berkeley, England. He became an orphan at the age of five, and an older brother took care of him. After an apprenticeship with a local surgeon, he studied for two years under John Hunter, a prominent surgeon in London. In 1772, Jenner returned to Berkeley and settled into the comfortable role of country doctor. He played the violin in a musical club, wrote light verse, and observed bird migration. He helped identify zoological specimens collected by **Captain Cook** on his first voyage to the Pacific. Jenner was offered the post of naturalist on Cook's second voyage, but he declined.

Jenner turned his attention to **smallpox**, an often-fatal disease. Those who did survive were often left blind, deaf, or facially disfigured with pockmarks. Jenner knew that survivors never fell victim to smallpox a second time. In fact, at the time, some parents exposed their children to mild cases of the disease to give them immunity from the more deadly strain. However, the strategy could be fatal if the disease came at full intensity.

Jenner investigated stories that milkmaids who contracted cowpox, a harmless disease, were forever immune to smallpox. For twenty years, he checked cases of smallpox or cowpox around the village. By 1796, he felt confident enough to try a dangerous experiment. He removed some matter from a blister on the hand of Sarah Nelmes, who had cowpox. He injected the fluid in the arm of an eight-year-old boy, James Phipps. The boy came down with a slight fever from cowpox. Six weeks later, on July 1, 1796, Jenner intentionally gave the boy smallpox. The boy showed no ill effects.

Jenner coined the word *vaccination* for his procedure, basing it on the Latin word *vacca*, for cow. For the next two years, Jenner met opposition from the scientific community. The London Smallpox Hospital refused to test his remedy. The English Royal Society refused to publish his report. In 1798, he printed a seventy-five-page book about his discovery. It caused an immediate sensation. Within eighteen months, twelve thousand people in London were vaccinated, including the royal family. Doctors, however, did not rush to honor him.

After a year in London, Jenner returned to the life of a country doctor. In 1802, Parliament voted him a sum of ten thousand pounds—a very large sum of money at the time—and Jenner lived comfortably until the end of his life. In the 1970s, the World Health Organization made a successful worldwide effort to eradicate the smallpox virus. No new cases have been reported since 1980.

English chemist **JOHN DALTON** was a precocious student who received training from his father and at a Quaker elementary school. He began teaching at the school at the age of twelve. In 1793 he moved to Manchester and taught science at a Presbyterian college. His first scientific interest was weather. He built homemade weather gauges and recorded readings in a daily log. In 1793, he wrote *Meteorological Observations and Essays*. It was one of the first scientific approaches to weather. Dalton collected 200,000 weather observations during his lifetime. He proved that rain forms because of falling temperature and not from changing atmospheric pressure. He observed **auroras** (northern lights) and concluded that the Earth's magnetism played a role in their formation.

Both Dalton and his brother were colorblind. In 1794, Dalton gave the first scientific study of this condition, "Extraordinary Facts Relating to the Vision of Colors," to a group of scientists that met in Manchester.

At the time, weather studies led to an interest in the atmosphere and gases. One important result was **Dalton's law of partial pressures**: The total pressure of a mixture of gases is equal to the sum of the pressures that each gas would exert if it alone occupied the whole volume. He collected methane (marsh gas) and found that it was made of carbon and hydrogen always in the ratio of 3 to 1 by weight. He was the first to clearly express the **law of definite proportions**: elements in the same compound always occur by weight in the same simple numerical ratios.

Dalton's most important contribution to science was his **atomic theory**. He put forth reasoned arguments that matter is composed of small, indivisible atoms. Atoms of the same element are identical. Atoms of different elements differ from one to another, especially in weight. In addition, atoms chemically combine in simple ratios to give molecules.

Dalton announced his atomic theory in 1803, and followed five years later with his book, *New System of Chemical Philosophy*. He answered the criticism it generated so reasonably that he overcame any personal attacks. Chemists quickly accepted his atomic theory.

Because of his Quaker beliefs, Dalton avoided any personal glory. Friends arranged for an audience with King William IV of England, but Dalton declined because he would have to wear court clothes that included a sword. As a Quaker he could not carry a weapon or wear richly colored garments. In 1832, Oxford University awarded him a doctor's degree.

Although Dalton became famous as a chemist, he spent his entire life as either a teacher or private tutor. In 1833, the king gave him a retirement pension of 150 pounds a year.

GEORGES CUVIER was born in Switzerland but became a French citizen when his birthplace was annexed to France in 1793. He attended Caroline Academy near Stuttgart, Germany. A fine student, he majored in administration but also studied anatomy. After serving as a tutor for a French family, he earned a post at the Museum of Natural History in Paris as assistant professor of animal anatomy.

In 1800, Cuvier became a professor at the College of France. By then, he no longer accepted the idea that all life could be organized into a single linear classification system, from the simplest organisms to humans. Instead, Cuvier proposed four separate divisions, or *phyla:* vertebrates, mollusks, articulates (jointed animals), and radiata (everything else). Cuvier argued that structures such as teeth and claws identified what kind of food animals ate. One night one of his students dressed up in a devil's costume. He sneaked into the professor's room and whispered, "Wake up. I have come to eat you." Cuvier looked at the devil's horns and said, "Creatures with horns and hooves eat grass. You cannot eat me."

Using his knowledge of anatomy, Cuvier reconstructed fossil animals from a limited number of bones. He could project the shape of missing bones by those nearby, and from them the rest of the skeleton. In 1812, he exhibited a pterodactyl, an ancient flying reptile. Cuvier's book, *The Animal Kingdom* (1817), applied his system of classification to fossil remains. Cuvier founded both the disciplines of **comparative anatomy** and **paleontology**, the science of fossils.

In his research, Cuvier observed that the deeper the fossils and the older the rock, the more the fossils differed in structure from those in more recent formations. Rather than interpreting this as evidence for evolution, Cuvier believed animals matched their habitat so exactly they could not survive changes to the environment. He suggested that catastrophes such as floods periodically inundated the Earth. The last catastrophe, Cuvier believed, was the Flood described in the Bible's book of Genesis. These upheavals caused mass destruction of animal life. The **theory of catastrophes** as he envisioned it is no longer accepted, but modern scientists recognize that events such as great ice ages and meteor impacts have caused mass extinctions.

At the same time he was pursuing his scientific work, Cuvier was a force in the public and political life of France. He managed to remain in high government posts despite the rapidly changing political situation. He served both Napoleon before he abdicated and Louis XVIII after the restoration of the monarchy. Cuvier filled increasingly important roles in public education and was in charge of reorganizing French higher education.

As a youth, **ALEXANDER VON HUMBOLDT** was a restless and lackluster student. However, a year at the University of Göttingen (1789) gave him an interest in botany, and he began collecting plants. While attending the mining academy at Freiberg (1790–1792), he worked mornings in the mines, attended classes during the afternoon, and in the evening searched the countryside for plants. He was employed as a mining engineer until the death of his mother in 1796. Then his inheritance made it possible for him to indulge his interest in exploration.

In 1799, he financed a scientific expedition to South America entirely with his own funds. He and a companion covered more than six thousand miles. They traced the path of the Orinoco River, collected plant specimens, took latitude and longitude readings, and measured temperature, pressure, and magnetic intensity. The two men showed enormous physical endurance in the intense heat, stifling humidity, and clouds of mosquitoes. Their food spoiled and they had to eat ground-up cocoa beans. After a visit to Cuba, they set out again, this time to the

highlands of South America. They climbed the **Andes Mountains**. Humboldt's ascent to 19,280 feet on Chimborazo Mountain remained a record climb for thirty years. During his trek, he suffered from mountain sickness and identified it as being caused by a lack of oxygen.

Upon his return to Europe, Humboldt settled in Paris because of its stimulating intellectual environment. His South America expedition supplied him with data for thirty books that he wrote over the next twenty-five years. He showed the relationship between geography and climate and the plants and animals that lived in a region. His study of **volcanoes** showed that the Earth's crust experiences continuous change. He identified the **Humboldt Current**, a cold-water current in the southeast Pacific Ocean, off the coast of Chile.

Humboldt had a knack for recognizing and encouraging new talent. He influenced the young **Simón Bolívar** to lead the struggle for South American freedom from Spain. A discussion with the American artist **Samuel F. B. Morse** about the French semaphore messaging system sparked Morse's interest in the possibility of developing a telegraph system using an electric current and a code.

By 1827, von Humboldt had exhausted his inheritance. He returned to Berlin, where he earned a living as a tutor and by giving public lectures. He visited Paris once a year and renewed old acquaintances. He convinced England, France, and Germany of the importance of international scientific collaboration. One such effort identified the Sun as the cause of **magnetic storms.**

At age sixty-five, Humboldt **popularized science** by writing *Kosmos*, a scientific encyclopedia. Humboldt died at age ninety, shortly after finishing the fifth and final book of *Kosmos*.

Mathematician, astronomer, and physicist **CARL FRIEDRICH GAUSS** established the **fundamental theorem in arithmetic**: every whole number is prime or can be written as the product of primes in one and only one way. Born to poor parents, the son of a gardener and a servant girl in Brunswick, Germany, Gauss was a child prodigy with a fascination for numbers. At age three, he corrected his father's calculation of the salary due other gardeners. Gauss's uncle convinced Duke Ferdinand to pay for the boy's education at the University of Göttingen.

Although he was foremost a mathematician, Gauss made breakthroughs in magnetism, astronomy, and **geodesy** (the size and shape of the Earth). His first public triumph came in 1801. On the first day of that year, Italian astronomer Giuseppe Piazzi glimpsed a dim planet that disappeared into the glare of the daytime sky. Astronomers had too few observations to calculate its orbit. Gauss calculated its orbit with the method of least squares, a procedure he invented that is still used today to fit a trend line to data. Astronomers recovered the object on December 7, 1801, in a position Gauss predicted. The body was **Ceres**, the first asteroid to be discovered.

Through the influence of Alexander von Humboldt (see no. 34), Gauss became director of the Göttingen observatory. He remained there for the rest of his life. At Göttingen, Gauss developed accurate surveying techniques. He also invented a **heliotrope**, a series of mirrors and a small telescope that surveyed the Earth by the straight lines of the Sun's rays. In 1833, Gauss built the first observatory designed specifically to measure the Earth's magnetism. He showed that the Earth's magnetic poles did not lie at the geographic poles. He built an electromagnet relay for sending signals between his home and the observatory, a distance of five thousand feet. It was the **first telegraph**, but he did not consider the invention of sufficient importance to publicize it. He postponed for thirty years publishing his theories of non-Euclidean geometry.

Throughout his life, Gauss learned languages to exercise his mind. At age sixty, he learned Russian. By applying mathematical analysis to financial matters, he made a fortune through investments. Gauss was deeply religious and conservative. Despite his income, he lived a simple life.

After his death, the force of a magnetic field was named the **gauss** in his honor. The bell-shaped probability curve is called the **Gaussian distribution**. During his lifetime, Gauss was asked to name the great mathematicians. He named Archimedes (see no. 5) and Isaac Newton (see no. 20). Today, his name is added to the list.

JOSEPH-LOUIS GAY-LUSSAC grew up during the dangerous times of the French Revolution. He attended École Polytechnique and graduated in 1800. Two years later, he made one of his most important discoveries. **Gay-Lussac's law** states that given an equal rise in temperature, all gases expand by the same amount if pressure is kept constant. This law led to a **key principle of chemistry**: equal volumes of different gases at the same temperature and pressure contain equal numbers of atoms or molecules.

On August 24, 1804, Gay-Lussac and French chemist **Jean-Baptiste Biot** made one of the first hydrogen balloon ascents for scientific study. Later, Gay-Lussac took a solo flight to 23,000 feet, an altitude record that held for fifty years. He captured samples of air at elevations higher than the Alps and measured the Earth's magnetic field. During the next two years, he traveled with **Alexander von Humboldt** (see no. 34) and measured the Earth's magnetism.

In 1808, Gay-Lussac found that gases combined to form compounds in volumes related by small whole numbers. Two volumes of hydrogen combined with one volume of oxygen to produce water. This observation helped reveal chemical formulas for compounds. Water is H_2O, with 2 representing that twice as many hydrogen atoms compared to oxygen atoms are present in the molecule. In 1811, Gay-Lussac and his friend Jacques Thénard succeeded in finding the composition of sugar, $C_{12}H_{22}O_{11}$: twelve carbon atoms, twenty-two hydrogen atoms, and eleven oxygen atoms.

During this time, the Institut de France gave the Napoleon Prize to Englishman Humphry Davy for his discovery of new elements. Napoleon was alarmed that a citizen of a rival country won the award. He provided Gay-Lussac with funds to restore France's honor. Gay-Lussac and Thénard treated boron oxide with the more active potassium and freed the new element boron. Gay-Lussac also named the element **iodine**, from a Greek word for its violet vapors. He investigated iodine's properties so thoroughly that he is often credited with its discovery. Gay-Lussac's work pleased Napoleon, and he saw that Gay-Lussac received an appointment as professor of physics at the **Sorbonne.**

The great French chemist Antoine-Laurent Lavoisier (see no. 29) had believed that all acids contained oxygen. Gay-Lussac investigated prussic acid (hydrogen cyanide) and showed that it contained no oxygen. His analysis showed that the essential element in acids is hydrogen, not oxygen. In analytical chemistry, Gay-Lussac invented the process of **titration**, in which the concentration of an acid in a solution can be found by the careful addition of an exact amount of a known base until the acid is neutralized.

In 1831, Gay-Lussac was elected to the French Chamber of Deputies. In 1839 he entered the Chamber of Peers and served as a lawmaker until his death in Paris in 1850.

HUMPHRY DAVY was born in Cornwall, England. As a boy he preferred fishing and exploring the English countryside to studying, and he did not do well in school. However, as a young man he become an apprentice to an apothecary and developed an interest in chemistry. In 1799, Davy became an assistant at a laboratory studying the medical uses of gases. Davy developed new gases and discovered the respiratory effects of **nitrous oxide** (laughing gas). Inhaling it caused unpredictable emotional behavior, such as crying or laughing. Davy suggested it could be used to deaden pain.

At this time, chemists suspected that several ores contained new metals, but they had been unable to separate the metals from the compounds. Davy believed electricity would pry apart molecules that resisted other methods. He made a battery with 250 cells, the largest in existence, and sent its current through potash. A silvery metal collected at one of the electrodes. Davy could barely contain his joy at his discovery. He called the new element **potassium**. A week later he freed a metal from soda ash and called it **sodium**. He also discovered **barium, strontium, calcium**, and **magnesium**. No other chemist had discovered so many elements so quickly.

Davy gave public lectures about his discoveries. He included dramatic displays of electricity and exploding gases. Because of his personal charm and showmanship, he became one of England's best-known scientists. He wrote two books: *Elements of Chemical Philosophy* (1812) and *Elements of Agricultural Chemistry* (1813).

In 1812, Davy was knighted. He married Jane Apreece, a wealthy widow. He could not carry a full workload because his lack of caution around chemicals had taken their toll; an explosion nearly blinded him.

In 1813, he selected the brilliant **Michael Faraday** as his assistant. When Davy took a two-year European vacation with his wife, Faraday accompanied him with a portable laboratory.

Upon his return to England, Davy developed the **miner's safety lantern**. He surrounded the open flame of a miner's lamp with a metal screen to absorb the heat but allow oxygen to pass to the flame. Explosive gases outside the lamp did not ignite. His invention enabled miners to work in previously unsafe conditions.

In 1820, Davy became president of the Royal Society. However, his years of working closely with chemicals had left him weak. Sometimes he could not leave his bed. Despite the hardships, he invented the bright arc light by sending a powerful current of electricity across the gap between two carbon terminals. It was the first attempt to use electricity to produce light. As his health deteriorated, Davy revisited his first passion and wrote *Days of Fly Fishing* (1828). He died in 1829.

JÖNS JAKOB BERZELIUS was one of the founders of modern chemistry. Berzelius studied natural sciences and medicine at the University of Uppsala, where he earned a medical degree in 1802. After a short time in medical practice, he became a professor of medicine and pharmacy at the College of Medicine in Stockholm in 1807.

That year Berzelius began working on the composition of chemical compounds. Using primitive laboratory equipment, he analyzed more than two thousand compounds over ten years. He calculated the proportion by weight of each element in particular compounds. He firmly established the **law of definite proportions**: elements making a particular compound are always present in the same proportion. Combining several discoveries by other chemists with his own work, he prepared the first accurate table of atomic weights.

Berzelius discovered the elements **cerium** (1803), **selenium** (1817), and **thorium**

(1828), and isolated other elements including silicon. Further, he proposed that atoms in molecules are held together by attractions between positive and negative static charges. Berzelius believed electricity freed metals from compounds by interfering with the static electric attraction between atoms. In this way, he gave the first modern explanation of the chemical bond. The role of static electricity in bonding atoms together remains an important principle of chemistry.

As the number of new elements grew, so did the confusion in how to represent them. In 1813, Berzelius used letters rather than drawings as symbols for elements. He said, "It is easier to write an abbreviated word than to draw a figure." Carbon was C, hydrogen H, nitrogen N, and so on. Should elements start with the same letter, a second letter would be used. Chlorine was Cl, calcium was Ca, and cobalt was Co. For gold (Au), silver (Ag), and a few others, he used letters from their ancient names. Most chemists began using these suggestions, and in 1860, they were officially adopted at the **First International Chemical Congress.**

Berzelius coined a variety of chemical terms. He applied the term **organic** to compounds produced by plants or animals, although the term now means carbon compounds. He introduced the term **catalyst** for a chemical that promotes a reaction without being consumed by it. He promoted his theory that groups of atoms—radicals—remained together during chemical reactions. He coined such well-known chemical terms as *protein* and *polymer*.

From 1821 until his death, Berzelius published a yearly summary of the state of chemical research. In 1835, at age fifty-five, he married a twenty-four-year-old woman. As a wedding gift, the king of Sweden made him a baron.

MICHAEL FARADAY, son of a poor London blacksmith, received only the basics of an education from a church Sunday school. As a youth, he served as an apprentice to a bookbinder, and was able to increase what little education he had received. He read the science books left at the store and repeated some of the electrical experiments.

One day, a customer gave Faraday tickets to English scientist Humphry Davy's lectures. Faraday took notes, bound them in book form, and sent them to Davy with a request for a job. He began working as Davy's laboratory assistant at the Royal Institution in 1813.

In 1821, Faraday married Sarah Barnard. They lived in an attic apartment above the Royal Institution so he could stay close to his laboratory. That year he built the first crude electric motor to change an electric current into mechanical motion. The opposite feat of changing mechanical action into electricity was more important to scientists because they could produce electricity only with batteries. Ten years passed before he made the discovery of **electromagnetic induction**: Motion of either electricity or magnetism will produce the other. He built the first electric generator. He also learned how to change the voltage of a current with a transformer. Faraday invented the three essential devices that made the electric age possible: **motor, generator,** and **transformer**.

Because he had only limited mathematical education, Faraday introduced visual pictures, such as lines of force and magnetic and electric fields, rather than mathematical equations to express his ideas. He showed that a strong magnetic field would twist polarized light. Faraday believed in a unity of the forces of nature. He proved there are connections between chemistry and electricity, electricity and magnetism, and magnetism and light.

In the field of chemistry, Faraday succeeded in changing "permanent" gases into liquids. He discovered the carbon compound benzene, which proved to be important in the synthetic dye and perfume business. Faraday showed a relationship between chemistry and electricity: the amount of an element freed as electricity passes through a compound is proportional to the electricity applied.

Despite his fame and accomplishments, Faraday lived a humble life. He never patented his inventions and survived on a small salary from the Royal Institution. He remembered his own childhood of poverty and gave free Christmas talks about science to youngsters. He published the first science book written especially for children.

In 1862, Faraday gave his last lecture because of his failing memory. He resigned from the Royal Institution, and he and his wife moved into a nearby cottage provided by Queen Victoria. When he died in 1867, he could have been buried at Westminster Abbey, but he expressly asked for a simple funeral and an ordinary gravestone.

The English mathematician **CHARLES BABBAGE** is credited with conceiving the first basic design concepts for a programmable computer.

As Babbage was growing up, his father, a wealthy banker, allowed him to study at home, using the best European texts. Babbage attended Cambridge in 1810, but he was appalled at the decline of English science compared to Europe. While still a student, he began an organization to translate French texts into English for use in English schools.

In 1820, Babbage built a model of a mechanical device for repetitive calculations. His **mechanical calculator** used the mathematical shortcut of logarithms to multiply, divide, and raise numbers to powers. The machine, called the **Difference Engine**, won an award in 1823 from the Astronomical Society. Babbage appealed to the British government for funds to build a full-sized model. Over the next ten years, he spent 6,000 pounds of his own money and 17,000 pounds from the government, but the model was never completed.

However, Babbage had other projects that did reach completion. He produced a number of minor inventions, such as the **locomotive cowcatcher**, the **speedometer**, and an **ophthalmoscope** for looking inside the eye. Babbage was also active in many scientific organizations; he was a founding member of the Royal Astronomical Society and the Statistical Society of London.

Babbage applied mathematics to time and motion studies. A British commission contracted with him to investigate the pricing of mail delivery. The commonly held belief was that postage of an item should be based on its weight and destination. The idea of flat rate postage had been proposed by others, and Babbage tested the idea. He showed that the cost of weighing a letter, looking up the destination, and figuring the postage took more labor expense than a simple flat rate. In 1841, Britain established the first modern postal system with a penny stamp for a half-ounce letter sent anywhere in the country.

Babbage had abandoned the Difference Engine because he had conceived a much grander device, a fully functional **programmable "computer."** He envisioned five essential components. The store (memory) contained the variables to be operated upon as well as intermediate calculations. The quantities were brought into the mill (central processing unit) to operate upon them. The control (computer program) gave instructions to the mill. Babbage's friend, **Lady Ada Byron** (see no. 45) wrote the first computer programs. Input was by means of punched cards. Output was by punched cards or printer.

However, despite thirty years of work and an immense sum of money, the analytical engine was never finished. Babbage had a detached certainty that he would eventually be vindicated. The first computers became operational during World War II. Babbage's concepts had been almost a hundred years ahead of their time.

◆ **JOSEPH HENRY** was the greatest American experimenter with electricity between the time of Benjamin Franklin and Thomas Edison. Henry was largely self-taught. His interest in science began when a resident of his mother's boarding house gave him a book about science experiments. He immersed himself in high school textbooks, and then attended Albany Academy, a local New York college. After graduation, he became a surveyor, and then a teacher of science at the college.

In 1829, Henry improved on the design of the electromagnet, which had been invented by William Sturgeon in England. Henry used more turns of wire than Sturgeon had and insulated them with silk. Henry's first electromagnet lifted twenty-seven pounds. An electromagnet he made for Yale College lifted a record 2,086 pounds. In 1831, he built a small electromagnet and strung wires from his college laboratory to his home a mile away. Pressing a button in the laboratory caused the electromagnet to ring a bell. It was the first **electric doorbell** and embodied the principle of the telegraph. To maintain a strong current in a long wire, Henry devised the electric relay, an electromagnet that switched in the next circuit powered by another set of batteries. He freely assisted **Samuel F. B. Morse** in perfecting the telegraph.

In 1832, Henry became professor of science at the College of New Jersey (later Princeton University). Because of his teaching duties, he seldom published his findings promptly. He missed being credited with his invention and improvements to electric motors, generators, and transformers. He did discover and receive credit for the **principle of self-induction**: a current creates a backward electromotive force that acts against the current.

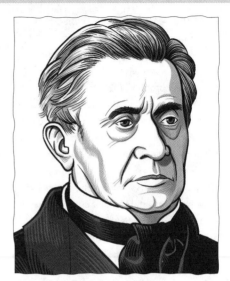

In 1846, Henry became the first director of the Smithsonian Institution in Washington, DC. In addition to housing the national museums in the Smithsonian, he made it a clearinghouse for scientific communication. He printed books about recent scientific discoveries and funded expeditions into the American West. During the Civil War, Henry served as scientific adviser to **President Lincoln**. On one occasion when Lincoln could not sleep, he worked late at the Smithsonian with Henry in experiments with signal lanterns.

Henry also conducted meteorological studies. He collected weather information by telegraph and produced the first map displays of atmospheric conditions. His work led to the creation of the **U.S. Weather Bureau.**

In 1875, Henry examined the first crude model of the telephone and encouraged Alexander Graham Bell to perfect the device. Henry never claimed credit for his role in making the telegraph or telephone possible, nor did he patent any of his inventions. In 1893, the unit to measure the force of self-induction was named the **henry** in his honor.

MATTHEW MAURY refined the study of the ocean into a science. Maury grew up on a Virginia farm but began his lifelong commitment to the sea when he entered the navy as a midshipman in 1825. In 1826, he began a four-year voyage that took him around the world. In 1836, he was promoted to lieutenant, but his career as a naval officer was cut short three years later by a stagecoach accident that left him permanently handicapped. The navy retired him from active duty and gave him a sinecure, a position with pay but no duties, as superintendent of the Depot of Charts and Instruments.

Maury accepted the position and began a second career as an **oceanographer**. He attempted to chart prevailing winds and ocean currents from old ships' logbooks available at the depot. They provided only limited information. He then designed improved logbooks and distributed them to captains of American vessels. By 1847, he published the first wind and current

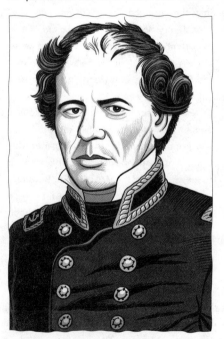

charts for the North Atlantic. He recognized the value of international cooperation and pressed for an international conference, which took place in 1853 in Brussels, Belgium. At the meeting, a uniform system of weather reporting at sea was instituted, and improvements were made in the collection of oceanographic information.

Maury studied the course of the Gulf Stream, whose existence had been identified by Benjamin Franklin (see no. 23). Maury mapped the path of the Gulf Stream, and measured its width, depth, and speed. Accurate knowledge of its speed and direction reduced sailing time between the United States and England. Maury gave it the classic description, "There is a river in the sea."

In 1855, Maury published *Physical Geography of the Sea*, the first textbook on oceanography. Cyrus Field of the Atlantic Telegraph Company asked Maury to prepare a profile of the Atlantic seabed. Maury made the first accurate chart of the ocean floor and discovered the Mid-Atlantic Ridge. In 1866, this plateau became the route for the first Atlantic telegraph cable from Newfoundland to Ireland.

The navy raised Maury to the rank of commander, but at the start of the **Civil War** in 1861, he returned to Virginia. He became head of coast, harbor, and river defenses for the Confederate navy. After the war ended, Maury went into self-imposed exile for two years in Mexico and then England. He returned to the United States in 1868 and taught meteorology at Virginia Military Institute, a post he held until his death.

Maury is known as the **pathfinder of the seas**, and his system of recording oceanographic data is still used today. His Depot of Charts and Instruments became the U.S. Naval Observatory and Hydrographic Office.

At the insistence of his father, **LOUIS AGASSIZ** went to school and earned a medical degree. Yet he had a passion for natural science that he could not deny. In his early twenties, he traveled to Paris to study comparative anatomy with Georges Cuvier. In 1832, Agassiz became professor of natural history at Neuchâtel, Switzerland. He made a monumental study of **fossil fish** that earned great acclaim.

Many naturalists of Agassiz's era believed that conditions on the Earth had remained uniform throughout the ages. Agassiz disagreed. He spent his summer months exploring **glaciers** to settle the question as to whether they moved. Agassiz drove stakes in a straight line across the ice. When he returned two years later, the glacier had carried the stakes down the mountain. Enormous boulders, some as large as houses, dotted valley floors. They were of a type of stone found only in the mountains. Agassiz explained that boulders embedded in the moving glacier had been carried to the valleys and dropped when a warmer climate melted the ice.

Agassiz faced a scientific community that was reluctant to believe that a great **Ice Age** had once existed. However, the evidence Agassiz amassed proved there had indeed once been a great Ice Age, and that change on the Earth over time had been extensive.

In 1846, Agassiz came to the United States on a lecture tour. He settled in Boston and was appointed professor of zoology at Harvard the following year. In 1850, he married Elizabeth Cabot Cary, and in 1861, he became a United States citizen. In 1862, he published *Contributions to the Natural History of the United States*, an exhaustive study of the American natural environment.

Agassiz believed Ice Age glaciers were a major source of change to the Earth's surface. When glaciers melted, they created most of the Earth's freshwater lakes. Glaciers had carved out the five Great Lakes of North America. In Minnesota, Agassiz discovered the remains of a sixth Great Lake. He traced out the shoreline broken here and there by deltas of rivers that had once flowed into the lake. The "ghost" lake was called **Lake Agassiz** in his honor.

Agassiz was the most prominent American biologist to oppose Darwin's theory of evolution. Agassiz agreed that environmental events could cause the extinction of species, but he argued that they could not give rise to new ones. He believed new species came about independently as special creations.

Agassiz was the best-known science teacher of the 1800s. He trained a generation of naturalists; he discouraged the use of books and instead insisted that students should be in contact with nature.

CHARLES DARWIN was born into a wealthy English family. His father had a thriving medical practice, and both of his grandfathers, physician Erasmus Darwin and china maker Josiah Wedgewood, were men of enduring reputations. Although Darwin studied medicine at the University of Edinburgh, and theology at Cambridge, he was drawn to the study of natural science.

In 1831, Darwin became the unpaid naturalist aboard the HMS *Beagle*. The voyage lasted five years and took him along the coast of South America and to islands in the Pacific. Darwin suffered chronic seasickness and spent as much time ashore as possible. There he collected plant and animal species and took extensive notes. During a five-week stay on the **Galápagos Islands** off Ecuador, he identified more than a dozen species of finches. Members of each species differed in the size and shape of their beaks and the food they ate. Darwin gave much thought to what caused the variations in the Galapagos finches.

When he returned to England in 1836, Darwin published some of his findings. His book, *A Naturalist's Voyage* (1839), demonstrated his attention to detail and clear style. Darwin then began to form conclusions about what caused the variations that existed between members of a sexually reproduced population. Darwin read *An Essay on the Principle of Population* (1798) by British economist Thomas Robert Malthus. According to Malthus, population growth always outstripped food supply, and famine, disease, or war kept human population in check. Darwin realized that other forms of life must be under population pressure as well. He theorized that because of random variation, some animals would be better fitted to survive and reproduce, despite environmental stress. These animals would pass on the traits that benefited their survival, and this would lead to the emergence of new species.

Darwin gathered evidence for his theory. In 1858, he received a paper from Welsh naturalist **Alfred Wallace** that essentially arrived at the same **theory of evolution** by natural selection that Darwin had reached. That year, he and Wallace published a joint paper on the subject. The next year Darwin published *On the Origin of Species* (1859). No scientific book has ever created such a furor or been so widely discussed. In his book, *The Descent of Man* (1871), Darwin took the step that Wallace had been unwilling to take—that human beings evolved from an earlier, subhuman form.

Darwin did not have the temperament for public debate. English scientist **Thomas H. Huxley**, known as Darwin's "bulldog," pressed the case for evolution against its critics. Religious opponents felt threatened by the theory, especially when they interpreted Huxley's support as an attempt to eliminate the need for a Creator. However, by the time of Darwin's death in 1882, most scientists had accepted the basic ideas of evolution.

ADA BYRON could be called the **first computer programmer**, because she conceptualized how to instruct a computing machine to perform an operation. Although Byron was the daughter of the famous English poet Lord Byron, she never knew her father; her mother left him as soon as Ada was born. Educated by tutors, she received advanced studies in mathematics from Augustus De Morgan, an accomplished London mathematician.

In 1834, Byron met **Charles Babbage** (see no. 40) at a friend's dinner party, and learned of his plans for an analytical engine, a mechanical computer. She was one of the few people who saw its potential and encouraged Babbage. In 1843, she translated a summary of a lecture Babbage had given about the machine. An Italian mathematician had written the article in French, and she added explanatory text to the complex treatise to help readers understand it. Byron's annotations were published with her initials to conceal that a woman had written them.

In a flurry of letters to Babbage, Byron predicted that such an analytical engine might compose music, generate graphics, and could have practical as well as scientific uses. She discussed whether a machine could be creative (use artificial intelligence). The analytical engine could be programmed by punched cards, which had been in use since 1801 to control weaving textiles on the Jacquard loom. She explained, "The analytical engine weaves algebraic patterns, just as the Jacquard loom weaves flowers and leaves." Once a program for a particular operation was entered on punched cards, it could be placed in the instruction stream of a different program to perform that particular operation. She recognized the usefulness of what are today are called subprograms and reusable code.

In 1835, Byron married William King. She became Countess of Lovelace when King was made an earl in 1838. As she raised their three children, she continued to correspond with Babbage. She encouraged him to abandon decimal-based calculations in favor of the 0s and 1s of **binary notation**. Byron focused on a single program, calculating Bernoulli numbers that are generated by an exponential series and used for statistical purposes. Her sequence of operations is regarded as the first "computer program." However, the technology of her time was not capable of translating her ideas into practical use.

From about 1843, Byron suffered from illnesses made worse by very strong medications that included opium. She died at age thirty-seven of cervical cancer. The first computer with the capabilities she envisioned was not constructed until the 1940s. A fail-safe computer language for use in unattended systems was developed by the United States Department of Defense in 1979 and named *Ada* in her honor.

English physicist **JAMES JOULE** was the son of a wealthy brewer who encouraged his son's scientific studies and supplied him with a home laboratory. Except for some instruction in science from chemist John Dalton at Manchester University, Joule was largely self-taught. In 1833, he took over the brewery at age fifteen when his father retired because of illness. Having the benefit of a private income, Joule continued his scientific studies.

Joule spent a decade making careful measurements of heat. His goal was to find the relationship between mechanical motion and heat. Although scientists agreed that mechanical motion could be converted into heat, they did not know the conversion factor. In one experiment, Joule measured the mechanical energy that went into turning a crank that he attached to paddles that churned water. As a weight fell through a measured distance, it turned the paddle wheel and stirred the water. He related the increase in temperature of the water to the distance the weight fell to calculate the mechanical equivalent of heat: dropping one hundred pounds through 7.78 feet

would raise the temperature of one pound of water by 1 degree Fahrenheit. Joule designed thermometers that could read 0.01 degree Fahrenheit and based his discoveries on very small changes in temperature. His experiment led to the first determination of the mechanical equivalent of heat—named **Joule's equivalent.**

Joule also conducted research and experiments on the relationship between heat and electricity. In his paper *On the Production of Heat by Voltaic Electricity* (1840), he worked out the formula known as **Joule's law**: heat produced is directly proportional to the resistance of the conductor multiplied by the square of the current.

Because Joule was a brewer, self-taught, and weak in mathematics, scientific societies rejected his papers. To attract attention to his ideas, he gave a public lecture and convinced a Manchester newspaper to publish the text of his speech. This generated enough interest that Scottish physicist **William Thomson** (see no. 50) attended his next lecture. Although only twenty-three years old, Thomson was well respected. With Thomson's backing, Joule's expertise was recognized. The Royal Society invited him to speak and, in 1850, elected him as a member.

Joule and Thomson worked together. They showed that when a gas expands freely, the temperature of the gas falls. The **Joule-Thomson** effect is the fundamental law behind refrigeration and air conditioning.

Joule's work established the first law of thermodynamics, usually called the **law of conservation of energy**: energy cannot be created or destroyed, only transferred or transformed from one object to another.

Joule remained an amateur scientist all of his life. The metric unit for work and energy, the **joule,** was named in his honor.

◆ **JEAN FOUCAULT** was a French physicist known for his experiments demonstrating the rotation of the Earth on its axis and determining the **velocity of light**. As a young man, Foucault completed medical studies but did not succeed as a physician because he could not tolerate seeing patients suffer during surgery. Instead, he became a science reporter for a newspaper.

Foucault's interest in physics, particularly the movement of light, led him to work with French scientist **Armand Fizeau**, who attempted to measure the speed of light on land. In Fizeau's device, light passed through a gap in a rapidly rotating toothed wheel. Foucault realized the method had an inherent error because the observer had to judge what speed of the wheel produced the brightest returned beam of light.

In 1850, Foucault designed an improved device. It used a rapidly spinning mirror. As light traveled to and from a distant mirror, the spinning mirror turned slightly, and the returning ray was reflected to one side. Measuring the angle through which it turned was more objective. His value for the speed of light was within one percent of the latest accepted value. Foucault also measured the speed of light in water. Scientists believed that if light were made of particles, light should travel faster in water, glass, and other dense media. If light were composed of waves, it would travel slower in water. In 1853, Foucault showed that the velocity of light was about one-third less in water than in air.

Foucault is best known for his **pendulum** that directly reveals the rotation of the Earth. He gave the first public demonstration at the Pantheon in Paris in 1851. The pendulum had a steel ball that weighed sixty-two pounds and was suspended by a 220-foot length of piano wire from the ceiling of the dome.

A spike on the ball marked its path in sand on the floor. The pendulum that was set in motion continued to swing back and forth in the same plane relative to the Earth's axis. As the day progressed, the pendulum's plane of vibration appeared to rotate slowly as the Earth turned under it.

Foucault investigated the physics of a spinning wheel with a heavy rim. He showed that it resisted changes in its axis of rotation, but if forced to move, the motion was at right angles to the force. In 1852, he invented the **gyroscope**, a device that became important to self-contained navigation.

In 1855, Foucault became an astronomer at the Imperial Observatory where he developed a way to create a **silver-on-glass mirror**, which greatly simplified making large telescopes.

From that invention, reflectors began to overtake lens telescopes in size and light-gathering ability, a change that would become more evident in the twentieth century.

Austrian biologist **GREGOR MENDEL** discovered the **basic laws of heredity**. The son of peasants, Mendel survived a miserable childhood of poverty and hardships. His background prevented him from going to school regularly, so he was largely self-taught. At the age of twenty-one he entered the Augustinian monastery in Brünn, Moravia (now Brno, Czech Republic), and in 1847 he became a priest. He was sent to the University of Vienna for training in mathematics and science.

Mendel combined his interest in mathematics and botany in a detailed study of the characteristics of **pea plants**. One characteristic of pea plants is size. Some plants breed true from one generation to the next as dwarf plants. Some pea plants breed true from one generation to the next as tall plants. When Mendel cross pollinated true tall with true dwarf, the resulting seeds produced about one-fourth dwarf plants and three-fourths tall plants. Mendel saw that seeds from the dwarf plants bred true. Also, a proportion (one-fourth) of the original of the tall plants bred true. The rest were hybrid. They appeared tall, but their seeds

contained the dwarf gene, which could appear in successive generations.

Mendel studied a variety of traits other than size, such as color of seeds, shape of pea, and so on. By 1865, he had summarized his findings in two laws that became the foundations of heredity in humans. The first theorized that through the sex cells in humans, traits are transferred as separate and distinct units from one generation to the next. This law is called the **principle of segregation**. Mendel's second law, called the **principle of independent assortment**, stated that traits are inherited independently of one another. He proved that two genes exist for each trait. Each gene comes from a different parent and can be dominant or recessive. A recessive trait is hidden unless both genes are recessive. A dominant trait is visible even if only one of the two genes is dominant.

Mendel presented his results to the Brünn Natural History Society. In 1866, his lecture was published in the society's *Transactions*. He also sent a copy of the paper to Karl von Nägeli, a well-known Swiss botanist at the University of Munich. The mathematics mystified Nägeli, who dismissed Mendel's experiment as interesting but not very important.

Mendel had been appointed abbot of the monastery in 1868. The additional duties, combined with the indifferent reception his research had received, chilled his interest in further study. He died in 1884, a lonely and forgotten person.

In 1900, three botanists, working independently on heredity, discovered Mendel's writings and duplicated his findings. The laws were publicized that year, and all three botanists credited Mendel as the discoverer of the process of heredity. Mendel's work has become the basic doctrine of the study of genetics.

LOUIS PASTEUR grew up in the small town of Arbois where his father was a tanner. As a young man, Pasteur studied in Paris at the École Normale Supérieure and was trained as a chemist. After he completed his schooling, he became a professor.

In 1852, while head of the science department at Lille University, Pasteur investigated problems with the fermentation of alcohol. Pasteur followed the stages of fermentation with a microscope and proved that yeasts are living organisms. One type of yeast gave rise to alcohol, but another type changed the alcohol into lactic acid. Gentle heating of the alcohol destroyed the second type of yeast, thereby preventing souring during the aging process.

Pasteur's work with fermentation led him to experiment with disinfecting various foods with a heating process. He found that heating milk to exactly 135 degrees Fahrenheit kills the harmful bacteria. The discovery revolutionized medicine. Doctors would eventually identify the different bacteria responsible for different diseases and would take measures to kill the bacteria to prevent infections from starting. Pasteur's process—the treatment of food with heat to destroy the bacteria—became known as **pasteurization.**

In 1865 Pasteur investigated the disease of silkworms that was devastating the French silk industry. Pasteur established that germs caused disease in silkworms. His solution was to destroy all the silkworms and mulberry bushes they ate and start with a fresh crop. He proposed the **germ theory of disease** to explain the cause of communicable diseases and infections.

Emperor Napoleon III supported the creation of a laboratory for Pasteur in 1867. The next year at age forty-six, Pasteur suffered a stroke that left him permanently paralyzed in the left leg and arm. His next breakthrough came by accident when full-strength chicken cholera had grown weak while left in the laboratory during his annual two-week vacation.

Inoculating chickens with the weakened cholera protected them against the full-strength disease. It was the first vaccination for a disease since the conquest of smallpox a century earlier.

In 1881, Pasteur developed a weakened form of anthrax, a deadly killer of livestock. Veterinarians belittled his breakthrough until he made a dramatic public demonstration. Both vaccinated and nonvaccinated animals were given a deadly strain of the anthrax. As a result, all of his vaccinated animals survived, and all the nonvaccinated animals perished.

The climax of Pasteur's career was the development of a vaccine for rabies, until then an always fatal disease. This discovery led to the foundation of the **Pasteur Institute** in Paris in 1888, which he headed until his death. Although he never earned a medical degree, Pasteur's discoveries of pasteurization, the germ theory of disease, and his **development of vaccines** were major advances in the history of medicine.

WILLIAM THOMSON was born in Belfast, Ireland. His Scottish mother died when he was six, and the family moved to Scotland in 1832 because his father had accepted a position as mathematics professor at Glasgow University. Thomson began classes at the university at age ten! After completing advanced studies at Cambridge, he returned to Glasgow as professor of physics at the age of twenty-two and held the position for fifty-three years. At Glasgow, Thomson created the first physics laboratory in a British university.

Thomson believed information about heat, mechanics, magnetism, and electricity could be converged in one unified theory. He collaborated with James Joule (see no. 46) in proving a relationship between mechanical motion and heat energy. As heat is removed from a substance, atoms and molecules move more slowly.

This implies that there is an "absolute zero" of temperature—the point at which there is no motion of the atoms or molecules in a substance. Thomson calculated that this coldest possible temperature is –273 degrees Celsius. All motion of atoms and molecules ceases at this temperature. Thomson developed a temperature scale that began at absolute zero.

Scientists quickly adopted his scale because it simplified calculations governing energy conversions. In 1851, Thomson provided another landmark of science, the second law of thermodynamics: the universe as a whole is becoming more disorganized as concentrated energy sources change into the random motion of atoms and molecules that make heat energy.

In 1856, American businessman Cyrus Field employed Thomson as one of the technical advisers on his Atlantic telegraph cable project. Thomson's analysis of the line showed that a faint current could be carried through the 3,000-mile cable. He built and patented a sensitive telegraph receiver that responded to the reduced signal. However, his view did not prevail against others who insisted on a stronger signal. The line was completed in 1858 but failed after two months. After the American Civil War, Cyrus Field tried again and named Thomson the chief engineer. The first reliable cable was completed in 1866, using Thomson's techniques, and Queen Victoria knighted him for his efforts.

A frenzy of cable laying began between continents. Thomson held the patents on designs of the cable and receivers, and he became wealthy. In 1892, he became a baron and took the title Lord Kelvin. He enjoyed traveling and made several voyages aboard his 126-ton yacht, Lalla Rookh. He also designed and built a variety of scientific instruments, including mariners' compasses and an analog "computer" for tide predictions.

Thomson lived to see his ideas change the world. In 1960, the scientific world honored him by officially naming the absolute temperature scale the Kelvin scale, with K to represent a Kelvin degree.

English surgeon **JOSEPH LISTER** was the founder of **antiseptic surgery** and introduced strict rules of hygiene to hospitals to help combat infections.

When Lister was a young man, his father hesitated to support his son's decision to become a surgeon. The father believed the boy was too kindhearted to endure the cries of agony of patients being operated upon without painkillers. However, in 1846, Lister's first year of medical school, the introduction of ether as an anesthesia in England removed that barrier.

After earning his medical degree in 1852, Lister took a position in Edinburgh, Scotland. In 1860, he was appointed surgeon at the Glasgow Royal Infirmary. Glasgow was an industrial town, and a steady stream of workers with broken bones came to the hospital. Those with simple fractures usually survived, but those with compound fractures, where the bones protruded through the flesh and were exposed to the air, often died of infection.

Lister was disturbed by the number of deaths from infection that followed apparently successful surgery. He became convinced that something in the air promoted infection. He kept wounds covered and believed cleanliness suppressed infection. Although his methods caused a reduction in infection, he could not give a scientific reason for it.

In 1865, he read about **Louis Pasteur's** germ theory of disease (see no. 49). Lister began a determined war against microorganisms. He soaked surgical instruments and bandages in carbolic acid that killed germs but did not damage flesh too severely. He washed his hands thoroughly before entering the operating room and sprayed the room itself with a mist of carbolic acid. Within two years, he felt confident

enough to publish his methods, but they were not immediately accepted by the medical community. However, his own results were impressive; his antiseptic procedures reduced mortality from 40 percent to 15 percent by 1869.

In 1869, Lister became head of clinical surgery at Edinburgh. He began a series of writings and tours of Europe and America to publicize his findings. In Germany, he learned that doctors used heat to kill germs on operating instruments and bandages. Chemists developed less damaging chemicals to replace carbolic acid. By 1876, many countries had adopted his methods. In England, however, his discovery was still largely ignored.

To sway the opinion of physicians in London, Lister agreed to become head of surgery at King's College London in 1877. He performed surgeries that other doctors would not attempt because of their fear of infection. While he was criticized for endangering the lives of his patients, his successful operations forced doctors to reevaluate their opposition. Before he retired in 1893, he had the satisfaction of seeing the triumph of antiseptic surgery.

FRIEDRICH KEKULÉ studied to be an architect at the University of Giessen in Germany but switched to chemistry. He received his doctoral degree in 1852, and after a period of traveling, returned to Germany and opened a small private laboratory in Heidelberg. In 1858, he became a professor at the University of Ghent, in Belgium.

Because of his earlier training in architecture, Kekulé became interested in the actual **structures of molecules**. Chemists represent the number and each type of atom in a molecule with subscripts. The hydrocarbon methane, for example, has one carbon atom and four hydrogen atoms, and is noted CH_4. Kekulé reasoned the structure of methane to be a central carbon atom surrounded by four hydrogen atoms. Kekulé knew that chemical properties depend upon both the contents and structure of a molecule. Ethyl alcohol and dimethyl ether have the same type and number of atoms: C_2H_6O. However, Kekulé determined their different structures. He put the oxygen atom near the end of ethyl alcohol, but in the middle of dimethyl ether. Kekulé's chemical structures were quickly adopted by other chemists.

Kekulé was the driving force behind the **First International Chemical Congress** at Karlsruhe, Germany, in 1860. At the meeting, chemists from around the world agreed to use letters as symbols for elements and clarified other important concepts such as atomic weights. Following the congress, Kekulé wrote a chemistry textbook in which he gave the modern definition of **organic compounds.**

Until then, organic compounds were considered only those derived from the organs of living things. However, chemists had succeeded in making organic like compounds that did not exist in nature. Because all such compounds contained carbon, Kekulé suggested the term *organic* for any compound that contained carbon.

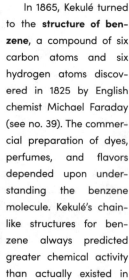

In 1865, Kekulé turned to the **structure of benzene**, a compound of six carbon atoms and six hydrogen atoms discovered in 1825 by English chemist Michael Faraday (see no. 39). The commercial preparation of dyes, perfumes, and flavors depended upon understanding the benzene molecule. Kekulé's chain-like structures for benzene always predicted greater chemical activity than actually existed in the molecule. After several weeks of fruitless efforts, Kekulé was riding in a horse-drawn bus when he began napping. He dreamed of the six carbon atoms as six little monkey-like figures that began whirling around one another. One monkey grabbed the tale of the other. Soon the six animals formed a spinning ring. When he awoke, he drew the diagram that appeared to him in the dream. Benzene was a ring. Kekulé's dream proved right!

Kekulé announced his structure for benzene in 1865. Chemists soon tested his idea and found it to be correct. Kekulé moved to the University of Bonn in 1865, where he remained until his death. He was raised to a noble in 1895 and added von Stradonitz to his name.

JAMES CLERK MAXWELL is considered the greatest physicist between the time of Isaac Newton (see no. 20) and Albert Einstein (see no 72). Maxwell was born in Edinburgh, Scotland, and grew up on his father's farm. As a country boy with a profound stammer, he suffered at the hands of classroom bullies when he began formal studies at Edinburgh Academy at the age of ten.

Maxwell spent time with an older cousin who encouraged his scientific studies. After doing well at the University of Edinburgh and then later at Cambridge, Maxwell accepted a position as a professor of natural philosophy at a college in Aberdeen in 1856.

Maxwell studied Saturn's rings from 1856 to 1859 and established that the rings were composed of a multitude of tiny solid particles, each an independent satellite of the planet. Calculations about the small particles in Saturn's rings gave him the skill to tackle the random motion of molecules in a gas. He combined the atomic theory of matter with the kinetic theory of heat to produce the **kinetic theory of gases**. From a few assumptions, he developed all of the known gas laws and predicted new ones.

Maxwell's experiments with color vision showed that the eye cannot distinguish between pure yellow extracted from the Sun's spectrum by a prism and yellow created by the combination of red and green. He proved that the retina of the eye receives three primary colors of red, green, and blue. In 1861, he used filters of three primary colors to take black-and-white photographs of a colored ribbon and then projected the images through the same three filters to produce the **first color photograph.**

After serving as a professor at King's College London for five years, Maxwell retired to his country estate in 1865 to experiment with gases and work on the problem of electromagnetism. In 1871, he came out of retirement to become a professor of experimental physics at Cambridge, where he established the Cavendish Laboratory in 1874.

Maxwell published his earlier theories and findings in *Perception of Colour* in 1860, and *Theory of Heat* in 1871. In his *Treatise on Electricity and Magnetism* (1873), he developed four concise equations that showed how electricity and magnetism are bound together as **electromagnetism**. All the previously known laws of electricity and magnetism could be derived from them. Maxwell's equations predicted the existence of an electromagnetic spectrum, of which visible light was a small part. **Heinrich Hertz** produced radio waves in 1887 as a direct result of Maxwell's work. Maxwell's equations are considered the most important development in physics during the 1800s because they showed that light is composed of electromagnetic waves.

Maxwell died at the age of forty-nine and received no public honors for his work.

Russian chemist **DMITRI MENDELEYEV** discovered a profound fact about chemical elements—their properties repeat in a predictable way. His great contribution to science was to create a table of elements that showed the trends and patterns in the properties of the elements.

Mendeleyev was the youngest child of a family of seventeen children. His father, headmaster of a local high school in Tobolsk, Siberia, died when Mendeleyev was thirteen. His mother managed to place him in a school for teachers in St. Petersburg before she died. In 1855 he graduated, taught for a year, and then returned to St. Petersburg for an advanced degree in chemistry.

Mendeleyev proved to be an exceptional teacher, and in 1859, the Russian government sent him to the University of Heidelberg in Germany for further study. In 1860, he attended the important **First International Chemical Congress** in Karlsruhe, Germany. After the congress, he returned to St. Petersburg, where he eventually became professor of chemistry.

Mendeleyev's students faced two problems. They had no good chemistry textbook in Russian, and they found it impossible to comprehend all the facts about each of the sixty known elements. Mendeleyev remedied the first problem by writing *The Principles of Chemistry* (1868–1870) in Russian. Then he tackled the problem of summarizing information about the elements. He wrote a note card for each element with information such as color, hardness, melting and boiling temperatures, and other properties. He cleared one wall of his office and hung the cards in rows. He arranged and rearranged the cards looking for a pattern to emerge.

Mendeleyev became convinced that the two essential properties were atomic weight and chemical combining power (valence). As the table took shape, Mendeleyev realized that the rows showed a regular change in chemical properties from highly active metals to relatively inactive metals, then to nonmetals, and finally to highly active nonmetals. This repetitive change in chemical properties gave Mendeleyev's important table its name, **the periodic table of the elements.**

In his final versions of the table, in 1871, Mendeleyev left gaps for elements yet to be discovered. For three elements, he predicted their properties in detail, including the atomic weights, compounds the elements formed with oxygen, melting and boiling temperatures, even their colors. Over the next twenty years, all three elements were discovered, and their properties closely matched Mendeleyev's predictions. It became clear that the periodic table was not merely a chance arrangement but reflected a fundamental property of the elements.

In 1893, Mendeleyev became director of the Bureau of Weights and Measures in St. Petersburg and held this position until his death. In 1955, U.S. nuclear chemists discovered element number 101, and it was named **mendelevium** in his honor.

WILLIAM PERKIN was the first person to start an entire industry based on a synthetic product. Born in London and educated at the City of London School, Perkin became interested in chemistry after attending lectures by Michael Faraday. In 1853, Perkin entered the Royal College of Chemistry, where he studied under the German chemist August von Hofmann. Because England had fallen behind the rest of Europe in chemical research, Queen Victoria had invited Hofmann to London to teach. Perkin became one of Hofmann's assistants.

Perkin built a laboratory at home so he could experiment during evenings and on vacations. Hofmann had suggested that the anti-malaria drug quinine might be made synthetically. It was extracted in nature from the bark of a South American tree, and the price had become excessive. During Easter vacation of 1856, Perkin gave himself the ambitious task of making quinine in his home laboratory. The project was doomed

to failure because the quinine molecule was far too complex to be made by the methods he had available.

Perkin experimented with aniline, a compound made from benzene and nitric acid. In one trial, he treated aniline with potassium dichromate. The reaction created a gummy residue, but a purple glint caught his eye. Perkin mixed alcohol to extract the colored substance. The alcohol turned the color of deep purple. He sent a sample to a textile company in Scotland and asked if it could be used as a dye. The owners of the fabric factory offered to buy it, provided Perkin could supply it cheaply and in quantity.

Although he was still in his teens, Perkin received the patent for his process in 1856. His father contributed his life savings to build a factory. With the help of his father and brother, the plant began operation within six months. Perkin marketed the **first synthetic dye** as aniline purple, although it became better known under the French name of mauve. Perkin soon became one of England's best-known chemists. When he lectured at the London Chemical Society, Michael Faraday came to hear him speak.

Over the next several years, Perkin made other discoveries, including the synthesis of glycine, the first amino acid to be made artificially; tartaric acid; and coumarin. Coumarin was a substance found in nature that gave newly mowed hay its fragrance. This set off a search for other artificial fragrances that began the synthetic perfume business. By then, Perkin had become an extremely wealthy person. In 1874, at the age of thirty-six, he sold his manufacturing plants and devoted himself to chemical research. With all his discoveries, Perkin helped establish the **synthetic chemical industry**. For his contributions to science, he was knighted in 1906.

◆ **WILHELM RÖNTGEN** discovered **X-rays** in 1895, and that discovery began a new era in physics. Although he was German, Röntgen attended a boarding school in the Netherlands and received his professional training in Switzerland. After earning a PhD at the University of Zurich in 1869, Röntgen did solid but unspectacular work at a variety of schools for the next twenty-five years.

During the 1890s, while he was a professor of physics at the Physical Institute at Würzburg, Röntgen began a series of groundbreaking experiments. He experimented with a cathode-ray tube that sent a stream of electrons through a glass tube. Substances placed inside the tube glowed when struck by the electrons. The stream of electrons could not pass through the walls of the tube. In November 1895, when he turned it on in his darkened laboratory, some nearby crystals glowed, although they were outside the tube. Röntgen reasoned that the cathode-ray tube gave off a second and more powerful invisible radiation. He used

the mathematical symbol X for the unknown and called them X-rays.

Aware that another scientist might make the same discovery and announce it first, Röntgen frantically experimented with the rays to learn their nature. The rays passed through glass, cardboard, wood, and thin layers of light metals such as aluminum. Heavier metals such as lead stopped them. Neither magnetic nor electric fields had an effect on the rays. The rays caused a barium compound to glow and exposed photographic film. As Röntgen placed a sample in front of the cardboard screen coated with barium, he saw a faint outline of his thumb on the screen.

Inside the outline was a darker shadow of his bones. He called his wife, and she held her hand still under the rays as he exposed a sheet of photographic film. Clearly visible were the bones of her hand and the darker shadow of her wedding band.

Röntgen announced his discovery in December 1895. On January 23, 1896, he delivered his lecture, "On a New Kind of Ray," to a largely disbelieving audience at the Physical Medicine Society of Würzburg. Their skepticism disappeared when he made an X-ray photograph of the hand of Albrecht von Kölliker. The developed film clearly showed the bones and joints of the elderly scientist's hand.

X-rays had an immediate impact on medicine. Doctors used the discovery to study the nature of broken bones and to locate foreign objects inside the body. Röntgen refused to patent the invention because of its medical implications. In 1901, he received the first Nobel Prize in Physics for his discovery.

Röntgen's discovery is sometimes used to mark the **start of modern physics** because it paved the way for the discovery of radioactivity and later quantum theory.

THOMAS ALVA EDISON pioneered the technology revolution by establishing the first research laboratory for applying scientific discoveries to practical inventions.

Born in Milan, Ohio, the youngest of seven children, Edison moved with his parents to Port Huron, Michigan, when he was seven years old. At age twelve, he got a job selling newspapers aboard the Grand Trunk Railway that made a run to Detroit.

One day, Edison rescued a stationmaster's young son who had strayed onto the railroad tracks. The grateful father taught Edison telegraphy. With the money he earned, he bought books about electricity. In 1869, Edison moved to New York City. His experiments led him to design a modified telegraph that printed stock prices on a strip of paper. He sold the invention, which would be quite useful on Wall Street, for $40,000.

Edison built his own workshop in Newark, New Jersey, and soon established the first U.S. research laboratory there. He headed a group of scientific workers who aimed to invent, patent, and produce inventions for profit. In 1876, Edison moved into a combination research laboratory and factory at Menlo Park, New Jersey.

Edison's first major Menlo Park invention was the **phonograph** (1877), a device that recorded sound inscribed as wavy lines on a tinfoil cylinder. Edison next turned to a practical way to produce **light by electricity.** After more than a year of trials during which he spent $50,000, success came when he used a scorched thread for the filament. On October 21, 1879, Edison sent electricity through the loop of carbonized cotton thread. It glowed for forty hours.

Edison's inventions soon made him a famous celebrity. He became known as the Wizard of Menlo Park. In addition to his scientific talents, he also proved to be a shrewd businessman. In 1882, he opened the first commercial electric light station in New York City. By the end of the decade, he had organized a number of companies to form the **Edison General Electric Company**; eventually it merged with its biggest rival to form the General Electric Company.

Toward the end of the century, Edison began experimenting with motion pictures. In 1903, his company produced *The Great Train Robbery*, the first movie to tell a story. Ten years later he succeeded in synchronizing sound from the phonograph with the movie projector to produce the **first talking pictures.**

In all, during his lifetime Edison held the patents to nearly 1,100 inventions, varying from a transmitter used in telephones and a new type of camera, to much simpler things such as wax paper. His home and laboratory are preserved as the Edison National Historic Site, in West Orange, New Jersey.

NATURALIST LUTHER BURBANK developed several hundred commercial varieties of plants. His work sparked a worldwide interest in **plant breeding.**

The thirteenth of fifteen children, Burbank was born on a farm near Lancaster, Massachusetts, and received a high school education at Lancaster Academy. His uncle was the director of a museum in Boston and introduced him to Swiss-American naturalist **Louis Agassiz**, who encouraged Burbank's enthusiasm for nature. When he was in his twenties, Burbank bought a seventeen-acre plot and began experiments growing potatoes. In 1871, he developed a large, hardy variety of potato that resisted diseases. Letters from three of his brothers who had moved to California convinced him that crops could be grown more easily there. He disposed of his land and combined the proceeds with his savings to finance his move to California.

Burbank bought a small garden in Santa Rosa, in northern California, and set to work. He had read Charles Darwin's book *Variation of Animals and Plants Under Domestication* published in 1868. Burbank

put into practice the idea that the characteristics of living things could be modified by artificial selection, hybridizing, and grafting. His garden eventually became a large experimental farm with nursery gardens, greenhouses, and plants from around the world. He carried on his plant hybridization and selection on a huge scale. He crossed native strains with foreign plants. To speed up the process, he grafted new sprouts on existing trees.

In 1893, Burbank issued a fifty-two-page catalog that contained more than one hundred of his new creations in fruits and flowers. In his fifty-year career, he produced more than a hundred varieties of fruit trees, twenty varieties of berries, more than thirty new grains and vegetables, and almost one hundred ornamental flowers and shrubs.

Burbank had no formal scientific training, and his record keeping failed to meet the standards scientists expected. In addition, he was initially unaware of Gregor Mendel's discoveries on heredity (see no. 48). When Burbank learned of them, he did not accept that characteristics of a plant were entirely determined by inherited genes. He believed changes caused by the environment could be passed on to the next generation, a concept for which no scientific evidence has ever been found. Despite being out of the mainstream of scientific methodology, Burbank's work convinced scientists that the living environment could be modified for the service of human beings.

Burbank's efforts helped establish the **Plant Patent Act** of 1930, although it was not enacted until after his death. In accordance with his wishes, he was buried under a Cedar of Lebanon tree as his only grave marker. He had planted the tree in front of his Santa Rosa cottage in 1893. In California, his birthday is celebrated as Arbor Day.

IVAN PETROVICH PAVLOV is best known for his study of the conditioned reflexes in animals. Pavlov was born in Ryazan, Russia, where his father was village priest. Young Pavlov attended the church school in Ryazan and then the theological seminary there. In 1870, he read Charles Darwin's *On the Origin of Species* and abandoned his religious career for one in science. He entered the University of St. Petersburg, where he studied physiology and chemistry under **Dmitri Mendeleyev**. In 1883, Pavlov obtained a medical degree from the Imperial Medical Academy; later he joined the Academy's staff as a professor of physiology.

Pavlov was interested in the interrelationship and communication between organs and the brain. In 1889, he surgically altered a dog's digestive system so the dog could eat but the food would not reach his stomach. Even without food, the stomach excreted gastric juices. Pavlov interpreted the results of this experiment to mean that the brain received messages from nerves in the mouth and then sent nerve impulses to the stomach to stimulate the production of gastric juices. He cut the nerve endings and found that without them the gastric flow stopped. Pavlov recognized that experimental tests create stress in animals that can alter experimental results. He took care to restore them to health and not to disrupt their normal functioning.

Pavlov conducted additional experiments between 1890 and 1900 that showed the role of the nervous system in regulating the digestive process. In 1897, he published *Lectures on the Work of the Digestive Glands*. By 1903, it was clear that his work was incomplete because he had not taken into account the action of chemical messengers such as hormones and enzymes for stimulating the action of organs. Nevertheless, in 1904, he received the Nobel Prize in Physiology or Medicine for his work.

In 1903, Pavlov began work that was even more important than his earlier discoveries. He experimented with **reflex action in animals**. A hungry dog salivated when shown food, an unconditioned reflex. Pavlov rang a bell each time the dog was fed until the dog associated the sound of the bell with food. Eventually, the dog developed a conditioned reflex and salivated from just the sound of the bell.

Pavlov's work in relation to human behavior and the nervous system also recognized the importance of conditioning. His discoveries had a profound impact on both medical science and psychiatry. As a practical application, he suggested that psychiatric patients would be better treated in quiet, low stimulation settings to avoid outbursts caused by unexpected, conditioned reflexes.

Pavlov thrived under the Soviet Union's Communist government. Certain government leaders recognized the usefulness of his work for mind control and brainwashing, although Pavlov avoided those areas of research.

English electrical physicist **JOHN AMBROSE FLEMING** invented the diode, the first device of the electronic age. Fleming was born in Lancaster, England, and after completing his university education, he studied at Cambridge and became an assistant to **James Clerk Maxwell** (see no. 53) at the Cavendish Laboratory.

In the 1870s, Fleming repeated the work done decades earlier by Henry Cavendish but had just recently been rediscovered. In the 1880s, Fleming served as a consultant to the Edison Electric Light Company in London. During the 1890s, he worked with **Guglielmo Marconi**, who had moved to England to perfect his wireless telegraph. In 1901, Fleming was at the transmitter in Cornwall, England, while Marconi set up his receiver in St. Johns, Newfoundland. Fleming keyed in Morse code for the letter *S*, and it became the first radio signal transmitted across the Atlantic Ocean.

Fleming became one of the first professors of electrical engineering, holding the position at University College from 1885 to 1926. He investigated Thomas Edison's

discovery that electrons boil away from a hot filament when electrons flow through it. Fleming developed the first application of the so-called Edison effect. He placed two terminals inside a vacuum tube similar to an electric light bulb. One terminal was a hot filament, the emitter. The other terminal was a cold receiver, the plate. When he gave the plate a positive charge, it attracted electrons from the emitter and encouraged their flow. When he gave the plate a negative charge, it repelled electrons from the emitter and suppressed electron flow. Fleming's device allowed electricity to flow in only one direction.

Fleming patented the device, which he called a valve, in 1905. It also became known as a **diode** (two electrodes) and **rectifier**. Normally, alternating current flowed both forward and backward, but a rectifier filtered out the backward flow. Fleming's valve converted alternating current into direct current. It was also a better detector of high-frequency oscillating current than the crystals used in radio receivers. Fleming's valve detected radio waves and converted them to weak direct current that could be played through a radio headset. It was the first practical radio tube. In 1906, American inventor Lee De Forest added a charged grid between the emitter and plate to encourage electron flow. With De Forest's triode to amplify the signal, voice communication by radio became practical.

Fleming was the author of more than a hundred scientific publications, the most important of which was *The Principles of Electric Wave Telegraphy* (1906). During his long life he saw the use of **vacuum tubes** in radio, television, radar, and electronic calculators. Although largely superseded by transistors, vacuum tubes are still used for high power demands and military equipment.

Scottish chemist **WILLIAM RAMSAY**'s great contribution was finding an entire family of noble gases that had been undetected in the atmosphere. Ramsay got his education at the University of Glasgow and later spent a year in Heidelberg, working under German chemist **Robert Bunsen**.

In 1893, while he was a professor at University College London, Ramsay turned to a puzzling question about nitrogen in the atmosphere. English chemist Lord Rayleigh prepared nitrogen in two ways, by releasing it from a compound and by removing all known gases from the atmosphere except nitrogen. The sample of nitrogen from the atmosphere had a greater density than the one from compounds. In 1892, Rayleigh wrote a letter to a scientific journal and asked for suggestions to explain why they differed.

Ramsay repeated the previous experiments and concluded that the atmosphere contained an undiscovered heavy gas that mixed with the nitrogen. He isolated a sample of this gas and found that it emitted spectroscope lines in a position that fitted no known element. In 1894, Ramsay and Lord Rayleigh announced that they had found a new element. They named it **argon**, from a Greek word meaning "inert." It displayed no chemical activity. It was the third-most-common gas in the atmosphere, behind oxygen and nitrogen. Argon composes about one percent of the atmosphere.

Ramsay realized that the periodic table had no gaps for a single element, but an entire family of new elements could be made to fit it. He searched for other inert gases. Years earlier, the English astronomer Joseph Lockyer had discovered helium, an element in the Sun that had not been found on Earth. In 1890, another scientist released a gas from uranium ore by treating the mineral with an acid. Ramsay put the two observations together and found that helium, the element in the Sun, also existed on Earth. At about this time, he received a sample of a gas from a natural gas well in Texas. He thought it might contain argon. He found that the sample contained helium, too. In 1898, Ramsay chilled a sample of the atmosphere until all of it turned into a liquid. Then he warmed it and trapped the gases as they boiled off. He found even more inert gases by this method. He named the gases he discovered **krypton** (hidden), **neon** (new), and **xenon** (stranger).

In 1900, radon, released by the radioactive decay of radium, was the last inert gas discovered. Although Ramsay did not discover it, he measured most of its chemical and physical properties. He continued to study helium and showed that it was a by-product of radioactive decay. In 1904, Ramsay received the Nobel Prize in Chemistry.

ANTOINE BECQUEREL was born into a family of French scientists. Becquerel studied engineering at the Bridges and Highways School (1874–1877). After he earned his PhD in 1888, he taught physics at the Polytechnique; in 1892, he served as research physicist at the Museum of Natural History in Paris. Both his father and grandfather had held the same post.

Becquerel studied naturally occurring phosphorescence of crystals: the absorption of energy by crystals and re-emission of that energy as light. Following the discovery of X-rays in 1895, Becquerel wondered if a phosphorescent material might also produce X-rays. He wrapped photographic film against light, then placed it in strong sunlight under a phosphorescent crystal. The crystal was a compound of potassium sulfate and uranium. If sunlight caused the crystal to emit X-rays, the rays would penetrate the paper and expose the film. When he developed the film, it was fogged. He modified the experiment by putting a coin between the

crystal and film. The developed film clearly showed the image of the coin, indicating that the crystal did indeed produce X-rays.

In March 1896, cloudy weather cut short an experiment Becquerel was doing with film. He put the film, still wrapped in paper, in his desk as he waited for clear skies. Because the bad weather persisted, he decided to develop the film. Becquerel found the film was strongly fogged. He realized that some sample in his desk had given off rays that caused the fogging. By a process of elimination, he discovered that pitchblende, a uranium ore, was the strongest producer of the unseen rays. Becquerel was astonished that the ore did not need to be exposed to sunlight to produce the radiation that developed the film. It was produced within the uranium atom.

In 1896, Becquerel published seven papers on radioactivity, a term invented by his friend **Marie Curie** (see no. 68).

Uranium was an obscure and little-known element until Becquerel showed that it produced radiation. The radiation was more penetrating than X-rays and more complex. Magnetic and electric fields deflected the radiation, an indication that the rays were composed at least in part of charged particles. In 1900, Becquerel measured the mass and electric charge of some of the particles. He intentionally carried a sample of radium, a newly discovered radioactive element, in his vest pocket for several days and reported upon the radiation burn that it caused.

In 1903, Becquerel shared the Nobel Prize in Physics with Pierre and Marie Curie in recognition of his discovery of **spontaneous radioactivity** and their study of its nature. Becquerel's son, Jean (1878–1953), also became a scientist, the fourth generation of physicists in the family.

Physicist **ALBERT MICHELSON** became the first U.S. citizen to receive the Nobel Prize in Physics. Born in Strelno, Germany (now Poland), Michelson moved to the United States with his parents when he was two years old. After attending high school in San Francisco, he went on to the U.S. Naval Academy in Annapolis, Maryland. After graduation in 1873, he became a physics instructor at the Academy.

In conducting some experiments, Michelson tried to measure the speed of light but failed in his effort. He found that he needed more knowledge of optics; to obtain this knowledge, he traveled to Europe and studied in Germany and France. When he returned to the United States, he resigned from the academy and became a professor of physics at Case Western Reserve University in Cleveland, Ohio.

In 1882, Michelson measured light's velocity as 186,329 miles per second; this value was exact enough to stand for thirty years. He then turned to the question of the luminiferous ether, a substance that scientists believed existed throughout space and carried light from the Sun to the Earth. Light traveling through the ether in the same direction as the Earth would have a greater velocity than light traveling at right angles to the motion of the Earth. Michelson designed a device named an **interferometer** to measure small differences in the speed of light. It separated light into two beams at right angles to one another. After reflecting from mirrors, the beams returned to the observer where, if their velocities differed, they produced markings called interference fringes. The experiment, done in 1887 with the assistance of American chemist **Edward Morley**, proved there was no motion of the Earth relative to the ether. Physicists concluded that the ether did not exist, and that light traveled at a constant speed regardless of the speed of the observer. Doing away with the concept of the ether was a boon to understanding how light travels through the universe.

In 1907, Michelson received the Nobel Prize in Physics for his development of sensitive optical instruments and the discoveries he made with them. During World War I, he rejoined the navy to design improved range finders. After the war, he attached a 20-foot interferometer to the 100-inch Mt. Wilson telescope in California, the largest in the world at the time. In 1920, he measured the diameter of the star **Betelgeuse** as three hundred times the diameter of the Sun. It was the first accurate value for the size of a star.

In 1923, Michelson began a new series of **measurements on the speed of light**. The average of several tests Michelson made, published after his death, gave a value of 186,278 miles per second. The latest scientific accepted value is 186,282 miles per second.

- One of the most influential thinkers of modern times, **SIGMUND FREUD** originated **psychoanalysis** and pioneered the **study of the unconscious mind.**

Freud grew up in Vienna, Austria, and lived there most of his life. After earning a medical degree at the University of Vienna, he initially concentrated his studies on the physiology of the nervous system and the effect of drugs, such as cocaine, on local nerves. In 1885, Freud spent time in Paris with French physiologist Jean-Martin Charcot, who used hypnosis to treat patients with ailments, such as paralyzed arms, for which there were no apparent physical causes. Freud was influenced by Charcot's belief that mental impairment can produce physical changes and cause severe illness.

Although he entered private practice as a neurologist when he returned to Vienna, Freud became interested in the psychological aspects of mental disorders. He developed the notion of the unconscious mind. He believed that the unconscious mind influenced a person's behavior. Freud experimented with hypnosis to help patients draw out forgotten experiences in the belief that making the unconscious conscious could cure mental illness. Although the hypnosis revealed painful memories, the patients could not recall them after the hypnosis ended.

Freud abandoned hypnosis in favor of free association. He allowed patients to fall into a state of relaxed consciousness. He encouraged a patient to say anything that came to mind and start a spontaneous flow of thoughts. Although the process was slow, it revealed deeply repressed memories that would normally have been kept from the conscious mind. The very act of talking about a problem provided relief. Freud developed this technique of *psychoanalysis*, a term he invented in 1896, to treat mental illness. Freud believed dreams also revealed the unconscious mind. In 1900, he published *The Interpretation of Dreams*; in addition to dream analysis, the book detailed his techniques for psychoanalytic treatment.

Freud's most controversial book was *Three Essays on the Theory of Sexuality* (1905). He argued that repressed sexual feelings dating from early childhood played a role in mental illness. The book created an uproar and ensured his becoming internationally famous. Later, he developed the **theory of personality**: that personality consists of three parts: unconscious impulses for immediate gratification (id), conscious curbing of those impulses to ensure self-preservation (ego), and internalized controls from family and society (superego).

Few of Freud's ideas received universal acceptance among medical doctors. Despite this, many concepts he developed entered popular culture, such as the **Oedipus complex**, the death wish, and slips of the tongue (now called **"Freudian" slips**).

In 1938, after Nazi Germany occupied his homeland, Freud, who was Jewish, left Austria and moved to London. He died there the next year.

JOSEPH J. THOMSON was the first person to discover a particle smaller than an atom. The son of a bookseller, Thomson was born near Manchester, England, and educated at a local college. In 1876, he received a scholarship to Trinity College, Cambridge. After a brilliant career as student, he remained at the university to teach physics. In 1884, he became professor of experimental physics at the university's Cavendish Laboratory.

In 1897, Thomson investigated "**cathode rays**," rays produced by tubes containing gases at low pressure. When attached to a high voltage, the tube discharged rays from its negative end, the cathode. Scientists questioned whether the rays were particles or waves. Thomson proved they were particles. In one experiment, the particles pushed a wheel along a track that he put in their path. Thomson reasoned that the particles had a negative charge because they curved out of their straight-line path under the influence of an electric field. He tested various gases in the cathode ray tube, and they all produced streams of particles with the same properties. He concluded that all matter contained these particles, which became known as **electrons**. He measured the ratio of charge to mass of the electron. By assuming it had a unit negative charge, he showed it to be almost two thousand times smaller than a hydrogen atom. It was the discovery of the **first subatomic particle.**

Because atoms are electrically neutral, Thomson imagined the electrons mixed with positively charged matter in atoms like plums embedded in a pudding. This was Thomson's "plum pudding" model of the atom. He assigned one of his students, **Ernest Rutherford** (see no. 70), the task of investigating atomic structure. With Thomson's help, Rutherford showed that the plum pudding model was incorrect. Rather

than being mixed in with the protons, electrons orbited outside the nucleus of the atom like planets orbiting the Sun. Thomson developed a way to separate atoms that varied only slightly in mass. He stripped away one of their electrons to give them a positive charge. When he sent the charged atoms through an electromagnetic field, those with the greater mass did not curve as sharply. In later experiments, he showed that atoms of the same element could differ in atomic mass. His experiments proved that one type of neon atom was 10 percent more massive than another type, although they were chemically identical.

Thomson enjoyed teaching and believed his research was aided by questions from younger minds. He urged his students to first experiment before reading about their subject so they would not be influenced by previous theories. Thomson received the Nobel Prize in Physics in 1906 for his discovery of the electron.

NETTIE MARIA STEVENS was a research biologist who showed that chromosomes determine the sex of an organism. Born in Cavendish, Vermont, of working-class parents, Stevens became a librarian and did not enter college until the age of thirty-three. In 1899, she received a BA at Stanford University, and a year later received an MA at Bryn Mawr College. After doing research in Italy at the Naples Zoological Station, and in Germany at the University of Würzburg, she returned to the United States. In 1903, she earned a PhD at Bryn Mawr in cell biology and stayed on there as a research biologist.

By then, she was deeply involved in the problems of **heredity**. Some researchers believed that an organism's sex was influenced by food and temperature during the early stages of the organism's development. Others believed heredity played a role, although they could not identify the mechanism.

In 1901, the work of **Gregor Mendel** (see no. 48) during the 1860s showing how two genes controlled each trait was rediscovered. With Mendel's work as a guide, Stevens studied the **chromosomes** in the cells of mealworm beetles. She chose to study these beetles because they had only ten large chromosomes, as opposed to the hundreds that were found in some insects. In the female, all ten were the same size. Males had nine large chromosomes and one small chromosome. In her studies, she established that chromosomes were inherited in pairs. The chromosome pair that determined sex had one from the egg and one from the sperm. If both were large chromosomes, the offspring would be female. If a large chromosome was paired with a small one, the offspring would be male.

In humans, the chromosomes that affect the sex were named by their shape, X or Y. A sex cell, egg or sperm, carried only one sex chromosome. In her 1905 paper, *Studies in Spermatogenesis with Especial Reference to the Accessory Chromosome*, Stevens showed that X and Y chromosomes were responsible for determining the sex of individuals. In an egg, the sex chromosome was always an X. Sperm cells were of two types, depending upon whether they carried an X chromosome or a Y chromosome. An embryo with XX chromosomes would develop into a female. An embryo with XY chromosomes would develop into a male.

Stevens's research career spanned only nine years (1903–1912), but she published more than three dozen research papers. Her work was not immediately accepted. Her research adviser at the college, **Thomas Hunt Morgan** (1866–1945), resisted the idea that sperm cells could be of two types. However, by the time of Stevens's death, the role of chromosomes and the genes they carried in determining sex was established, and her studies sparked a continued and intense interest in heredity.

GEORGE WASHINGTON CARVER was born into slavery during the Civil War on the farm of Moses and Susan Carver near Diamond Grove, Missouri. He and his mother, Mary, were abducted by raiders and taken into Arkansas. Moses Carver succeeded in rescuing the young child, but Carver's mother was never found. Moses and Susan Carver raised the frail George as their own, and he took their name. He was too slight for heavy farm work, so he did the laundry, ironing, and gardening.

Carver left Diamond Grove to attend high school and was nearly twenty-five years old before he completed his high school education. He won a scholarship to Highland University in Kansas, but he was later rejected because of his race. In 1889, he entered Simpson College in Iowa and then, in 1891, transferred to Iowa State Agricultural College. He graduated with honors in 1894 and received a master's degree two years later in **agricultural science**. He then joined the school's faculty but gave up the position to work with **Booker T. Washington** at the Tuskegee Institute in Alabama.

At the institute, Carver became Director of Agricultural Research. He found that the plot of land for his experimental farm had been planted in cotton for so many years that the soil was completely depleted of nutrients. He realized that poor Southern farmers faced the same problem. Carver worked to develop ways to restore the soil. He found that peanuts and sweet potatoes would grow in poor soil.

Because they were legumes with nitrogen-fixing bacteria around their roots, they restored nutrients to the soil. However, Carver knew neither peanuts nor sweet potatoes were cash crops. He remedied the situation by developing products that could be made from them. He developed three hundred products from peanuts, including cheese, flour, ink, dyes, and plastics. From sweet potatoes, he developed more than a hundred products including molasses, synthetic rubber, and glue.

Carver urged farmers to plant a portion of their fields each year in peanuts, sweet potatoes, or soybeans rather than cotton alone. Starting in the 1910s, farmers who heeded his message were spared devastating loses when a boll weevil infestation destroyed their cotton. As the pest became more difficult to control, other farmers tried Carver's methods. The peanut became the South's second-largest crop behind cotton.

By the 1930s, Carver was recognized as one of the world's greatest **plant scientists**. He published annual bulletins to offer farming advice. He outfitted a portable classroom in a wagon and took his message to poor farmers. Over the years, Carver turned down well-paying offers with other organizations and remained at Tuskegee. A humble and soft-spoken man, he played a major role in making the United States one of the most efficient food producers in the world.

◆ **MARIE CURIE** became the first woman to win a Nobel Prize and the first person to win two Noble Prizes. Born in Warsaw, Poland, Marie moved to Paris in her twenties to study at the Sorbonne. In 1894, she met French chemist **Pierre Curie** and they were married a year later. For her doctor's thesis, she investigated the radiation from uranium discovered in 1896 by her friend Antoine Henri Becquerel (see no. 62).

Marie Curie invented a way to **measure radioactivity** by the ionization of air that it caused. She tested various uranium compounds and found that the level of radiation they produced depended on the amount of uranium in them. She stated the revolutionary idea that radioactivity was not a chemical property—a property resulting from reactions between atoms—but instead radioactivity was a property of the atom itself. Some ores displayed radioactivity far out of proportion to the uranium they contained. What was the reason for this? She

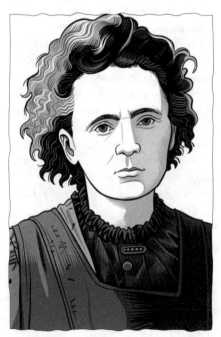

concluded that radioactive elements existed that had not yet been discovered. Her husband abandoned his own research to assist her. In 1898, they found the radioactive elements that had previously been unknown. They refined a new radioactive element from uranium that she named **polonium**, after her native country.

The Curies also detected another element in pitchblende, a uranium ore. For four years, she and her husband worked in a primitive unheated shed to separate the new element from tons of pitchblende. By 1902, they had one-tenth of a gram of the newly discovered substance, a sample about the size of a pinhead. It was enough to weigh and analyze, and they named it **radium**. Curie kept the vial of radium by her bed for the ghostly glow it gave at night. In 1903, the Curies and Becquerel shared the Nobel Prize in Physics for discoveries in radioactivity.

In 1906, Pierre died in a street accident. Marie took over his lectures at the Sorbonne and became the school's first woman teacher. In 1911, she received her second Nobel Prize; this one was in chemistry, awarded for her discovery of polonium and radium. During World War I, she stayed in France to build portable X-ray machines for field hospitals and ambulances. Her laboratory, the Radium Institute, opened after the war and she researched medical uses of radioactivity.

Marie and Pierre Curie had two daughters, one of whom followed in their scientific footsteps. Irène Curie (see no. 79) and her husband, Frédéric Joliot, worked together as her parents had done, and in 1935, they won the Nobel Prize in Chemistry. The Curies' daughter Éve wrote a best-selling biography of her mother shortly before Marie died of leukemia caused by exposure to radiation.

HENRIETTA SWAN LEAVITT discovered how to gauge intergalactic distances at a time when such distances were difficult to determine. Leavitt was born in Lancaster, Massachusetts, and graduated from Radcliffe College in 1892. She did volunteer work at Harvard College Observatory, and in 1902 she became a permanent member of the staff. As head of the photographic photometry department, she measured the brightness of stars photographed on glass negatives and identified those that changed in brightness. With her discoveries she doubled the number of known variable stars to about five thousand.

Leavitt became acquainted with a category of variable stars known as **Cepheids**. The first of them had been discovered in the constellation of Cepheus in 1784. Stars pulsated from bright to dim to bright again in a very predictable way. From one Cepheid to the next, the period could vary from about eighteen hours to as much as fifty-six days. However, for any particular such star, the period remained constant. In 1907, she began to suspect that the brighter Cepheids had the longer periods. However, she could not be certain of their true brightness because she did not know their distance. The only method to find distances of stars was by their parallax, the apparent shift of their positions as the Earth moved from one side of its orbit to the other. None of the Cepheids were near enough for their distance to be measured by parallax.

Leavitt extended her brightness measurements with photographs taken at the Harvard Observatory in Peru. She studied images of the two Magellanic Clouds, named after Ferdinand Magellan. These small, irregular galaxies were neighbors of the Milky Way galaxy but fell outside it. She reasoned that variations in distances among stars within the clouds were slight compared to their vast distance from the Earth. She identified twenty-five Cepheids within the Small Magellanic Cloud and plotted their periods against their maximum brightness. All of those with the same period had the same maximum brightness. Those with longer periods were brighter than those with shorter periods.

In 1912, she announced her **period-luminosity law**: a Cepheid revealed its true brightness by its period. Using this law, the distance of a Cepheid could be calculated given its period and apparent brightness. The next year, Danish astronomer **Ejnar Hertzsprung** accurately estimated the distances of a few Cepheids, and the distance to the others could then be calculated. The Small Magellanic Cloud was 173,000 light years away.

The yardstick of Cepheid variables that Leavitt discovered made it possible to measure intergalactic distances because Cephids are bright stars and can be seen at great distances. The period-luminosity law was the single most important means to measure the distance to a galaxy or cluster of stars in the first half of the twentieth century.

One of the greatest experimental physicists of the twentieth century, **ERNEST RUTHERFORD** was born and grew up in New Zealand. A very bright student, he received a scholarship to Cambridge University in England in 1895, where he worked under the great English physicist **Joseph J. Thomson** (see no. 65). In 1898, Rutherford became a physics professor at McGill University in Montreal, Canada. After nine years at McGill, he became head of physics at Manchester University in England.

Rutherford began investigating radioactivity in 1897, and in 1898, he showed that radioactive elements gave off three types of emanations, which he named alpha, beta, and gamma. He proved that alpha particles had the same mass as helium atoms, a charge of +2, and a speed in the neighborhood of twenty thousand miles per second. Beta particles were identical to electrons traveling at nearly the speed of light. Gamma radiations were electromagnetic rays even more energetic and penetrating than X-rays.

Although chemists believed atoms were indestructible and unchangeable, Rutherford showed that radioactive elements tore themselves apart and changed into atoms of an entirely different element. Although no one could predict when a uranium atom would break down, a large sample disintegrated at a very predictable rate. Rutherford invented the term **"half-life,"** the time for one half of the sample to be gone, to measure the rate of radioactive decay. For his study of radioactive elements, Rutherford won the 1908 Nobel Prize in Chemistry.

Rutherford used alpha particles as high-speed bullets to probe inside the atom. He sent them through a very thin sheet of gold foil. Most alpha particles passed straight through the foil. This indicated that atoms were mostly empty space. However, about one in ten thousand alpha particles bounced back as if they had struck an incredibly massive target. Rutherford proposed that the atom had a dense, central core that he called the **nucleus**. It contained most of the mass and all of the positive charge of the atom. Electrons circled the nucleus and carried the negative charge but only a small amount of the mass.

In 1914, Rutherford suggested that the simplest positive particle would be identical to the hydrogen atom with the electron removed. He called the particle a **proton**. In 1917, Rutherford passed alpha particles through nitrogen gas and knocked protons loose. The nitrogen atom that lost the proton became oxygen. Rutherford was the first person to induce a nuclear change. Newspapers called it **"atom smashing."**

In 1919, Rutherford became head of the Cavendish Laboratory at Cambridge, where he remained for the rest of his life. Rutherford had been knighted in 1914, and in 1931 he became Baron Rutherford.

LISE MEITNER discovered **nuclear fission** (the splitting of atoms into two parts of roughly equal size) and provided a scientific explanation for the process. Meitner was born in Vienna, Austria, and received a PhD from the University of Vienna in 1905. After she graduated, she went to Berlin, where she became the assistant of chemist **Otto Hahn.**

Meitner worked with Hahn at the Kaiser Wilhelm Institute for Chemistry in Berlin. However, as the first woman physics professor in Germany, she suffered gender discrimination. She was refused permission to work in the laboratory by their supervisor because she was a woman. She was forced to set up a small laboratory in a carpenter's workroom. Nevertheless, in 1917, she was named joint director of the institute with Hahn, and she was also appointed head of the physics department. In 1918, Meitner and Hahn announced their discovery of element number 91, **protactinium.**

In 1934, she and Hahn began to study the effects of neutron bombardment on uranium. They expected to see heavier atoms, but the bombardment resulted in lighter radioactive products. Before they could finish their work, however, Meitner was dismissed from her post because of her Jewish background. In 1938, she was forced to flee Nazi Germany. Early the next year, Otto Hahn published the results of their work. He found that one of the products from uranium was the much lighter metal barium. He did not list Meitner as a coauthor because her name had been banned from German publications.

Swedish physicist **Niels Bohr** (see no. 74) arranged for Meitner to continue her research in Sweden. Meitner realized that a captured proton caused the uranium nucleus to become unstable and split into two roughly equal pieces. One part was barium, and she calculated that the other part would be krypton. Meitner's nephew, Otto Frisch, worked at Bohr's laboratory in Copenhagen. The two scientists kept in daily communication by telephone as he tested her theory.

In 1939, Meitner published two papers about fission and became the first to state that uranium and thorium could undergo fission. As Meitner stated, the fission reaction produces a great amount of energy.

When Meitner added the masses of the products of the reaction, the total was less than a uranium atom. She asserted that the lost mass had changed into energy and calculated the amount using Einstein's mass energy equation, $E=mc^2$. She was the first to predict that a fission reaction could become self-sustaining by the neutrons that the reaction released.

Meitner's coworker Otto Hahn was awarded the Nobel Prize in Chemistry in 1944. Meitner, however, was not recognized for her contributions. In 1992, one of the transuranium elements was named **meitnerium** in her honor.

ALBERT EINSTEIN is recognized as the greatest scientist of the twentieth century. Born in Ulm, Germany, Einstein attended high school in Switzerland and became a Swiss citizen in 1901. He received his PhD from the University of Zurich in 1905. When he could not find a position at a university, he went to work in the patent office. He conducted his scientific inquiries after work and had a lively circle of scientist friends with whom he discussed his ideas.

In 1905, Einstein published his **special theory of relativity**; in 1915, he published his **general theory of relativity**. These two theories revolutionized science's understanding of matter, space, and time.

In the special theory of relativity, Einstein began with the premises that (1) laws of nature are the same for all observers in unaccelerated motion, and (2) the speed of light is constant in the universe. He concluded that time is relative (or not constant), and that the upper limit to speed is that of

light in a vacuum. He worked out the famous equation, $E=mc^2$, a relationship between energy, E, and mass, m, with c^2 representing the speed of light squared. The equation explained the vast amount of energy generated by the Sun and nuclear reactions.

In the general theory of relativity, Einstein explained gravitation as due to the curvature of space. He predicted that the gravity of the Sun would bend the path of starlight. Photographs taken during the solar eclipse of 1919 confirmed Einstein's general theory of relativity and made him world famous.

Einstein also did groundbreaking scientific investigations in what he termed the **"photoelectric" effect**. It was observed that light that struck certain metals knocked loose electrons. In addition, the color of the light controlled the speed of emitted electrons, and the brightness of the light controlled the number of emitted electrons. These observations were not consistent with the idea that light is composed of waves—an idea prevalent at the time. Einstein argued that light came in packets (later called "photons"), with each color having a certain amount of energy. This concept explained the photoelectric effect so thoroughly that scientists had to accept the idea that light had a particle nature, as well as a wave nature.

In 1914, Einstein had returned to Germany to become a professor at the University of Berlin. When the Nazis came to power in 1933, he was forced from his position; he emigrated to the United States and became a permanent member of the Institute of Advanced Study at Princeton, New Jersey. In 1939, he sent a letter to President **Franklin D. Roosevelt**, prompting the United States to begin the development of the **atomic bomb**. After World War II, Einstein became actively involved in the movement to abolish nuclear weapons.

Scottish bacteriologist **ALEXANDER FLEMING** discovered **penicillin**, the first antibiotic drug. The son of a farmer, Fleming could not afford to go to college. As a young man, he found work in London as a shipping clerk, and in 1900 he joined the army. In 1902, he received a scholarship for medical studies at St. Mary's Hospital, London University. In 1906, he earned his medical degree there and stayed on to teach in the bacteriology department.

During World War I, Fleming served in the medical corps. In treating wounds, he noticed that many of the chemicals used to cleanse bacteria from wounds also caused damage to the human cells. After the war, he returned to research and teaching at St. Mary's. He searched for substances that were toxic to bacteria but not to human cells.

In 1921, Fleming discovered a substance that he called **lysozyme**, a protein enzyme found in saliva and tears. Although it killed germs without damaging human tissue, the germs it killed were not those that caused human infections. Fleming's equipment at St. Mary's was limited. His laboratory was a roughly furnished basement room with an open window for ventilation. Using a jellylike culture in petri dishes, he grew staphylococcus germs that caused boils in humans. One day in 1928, he noticed that foreign matter had fallen into one of the dishes and begun killing the staphylococcus bacteria. He identified the foreign substance as *Penicillium notarum*, a mold similar to bread mold.

Fleming isolated the dark green mold and purified a bit of the active ingredient. He named it penicillin. The substance was deadly to bacteria that infected humans. It left protein unharmed, and when he injected mice with it, they showed no ill effects. Purifying small amounts of penicillin was more than Fleming could accomplish in his limited laboratory. He published his results in May 1929 in the hopes that someone could make it in larger amounts. The report aroused little interest.

Late in the 1930s, as England went to war with Germany, British medical researcher **Howard Walter Florey** researched possible ways to prevent infection from battlefield wounds. He and his brilliant assistant, **Ernst Boris Chain**, had a well-equipped laboratory at Oxford University. They came across Fleming's paper on penicillin and traveled to St. Mary's. Fleming gave them a sample of the mold. For ten years, he had kept it alive, transferring it from one petri dish to another. They confirmed Fleming's work, developed a way to mass-produce penicillin, and took it to America where it was made in great amounts.

By 1944, penicillin had become the best known "miracle" drug. In 1945, Fleming, Florey, and Chain shared the Nobel Prize in Physiology or Medicine.

NIELS BOHR'S great contribution to science was to develop a **"quantized" model of the atom**. Bohr was born in Copenhagen, Denmark, and attended the University of Copenhagen. After receiving his PhD in physics in 1911, Bohr went to England to study with physicist and teacher **Joseph J. Thomson** (see no. 65) at the Cavendish Laboratory. The next year he moved to the University of Manchester to work with physicist **Ernest Rutherford** (see no. 70).

In 1916, Bohr became professor of physics at the University of Copenhagen; officials then built the **Institute of Theoretical Physics** for his work and research. Bohr's motivation was to overcome an objection to Rutherford's model of the atom. Normally, moving electrons radiate energy. Why, then, didn't orbiting electrons in Rutherford's model lose energy and spiral into the nucleus? Bohr applied the quantum theory to answer the question. The quantum theory held that electrons could possess only certain discrete amounts of energy; energy in atoms is discrete like steps on a ladder, rather than smoothly distributed like a ramp. In atoms, electrons have certain energy steps, or orbits, and specific amounts of energy. They change orbits only by absorbing or emitting "packets" or quanta of energy.

Bohr also applied the quantum theory to spectroscopic lines. When elements were heated, they emitted a characteristic set of light bands visible through a spectroscope. Bohr studied hydrogen, the element with the simplest set of spectral lines. As hydrogen gas was heated, the energy bumped up its sole electron into a higher orbit. However, the electron could achieve the orbit only by absorbing a specific packet of energy. When the heat was removed, the electron fell back to its ground state and released the exact same amount of energy, thus causing the spectroscopic line of a certain color.

Bohr guided the course of physics in the first half of the twentieth century. He received the 1922 Nobel Prize in Physics for his investigation of the structure of atoms and the radiation emanating from them.

In 1939, Bohr visited the United States and convinced American scientists of the importance of **Lise Meitner's** (see no. 71) discovery of uranium fission. After he returned to Denmark, he was caught in the German occupation of his country and took an active part in the resistance movement. In 1943, Bohr learned he was about to be arrested by the Germans. He escaped by fishing boat to Sweden and from there flew to England and then to the United States. He went to Los Alamos, New Mexico, and took part in the development of the **atomic bomb**. Following the war, he became a strong advocate for the peaceful uses of atomic energy.

SELMAN WAKSMAN was born near Kiev, Ukraine (then part of the Russian Empire), and educated primarily by private tutors, although he attended high school in Odessa. After graduation he emigrated to the United States, where he attended Rutgers College in New Jersey. In 1915, he graduated with a degree in agriculture and went to work at the New Jersey Agricultural Experiment Station in soil bacteriology. The next year he became a United States citizen and received a fellowship to the University of California, where he received his PhD in biochemistry in 1918.

Waksman returned to Rutgers and the Experimental Station where he concentrated on the role of microorganisms in the soil. During the next twenty years, he published nearly four hundred papers detailing how microorganisms gave fertility to the soil and created humus by decomposing plants and animals. He became an authority on **soil microbiology.**

Waksman's expertise in soil bacteria became especially important when the properties of penicillin were publicized in 1939. He coined the term **"antibiotic"** (against life) for those agents that would kill disease-causing bacteria. Early antibiotics were types of protein that attached to disease-causing microorganisms and interfered with their ability to synthesize food. Waksman realized that penicillin was not a universal antibiotic. Years earlier, Danish bacteriologist Hans Gram stained bacteria with an iodine solution to make them visible through a microscope. When he washed the bacteria with alcohol, it removed the stain from some bacteria but not from others. This became a useful way to classify bacteria. Those bacteria that retained the stain became known as gram-positive, and those that lost it were gram-negative. Penicillin was effective against gram-positive bacteria but left untouched the gram-negative ones.

The bacteria that caused tuberculosis was gram-negative and resisted penicillin. Waksman noticed that the tuberculosis bacteria did not survive in the soil. To find the cause, he and his staff made a systematic study of more than ten thousand microorganisms found in the soil. In 1943, he found it in a mold of the streptomyces family, which he had been growing for almost twenty years. He extracted an antibiotic, and in 1945 he patented it as streptomycin. It proved effective against tuberculosis and other gram-negative bacteria such as pneumonia, spinal meningitis, and typhoid fever. From his extensive samples of mold and other microorganism, he isolated several other antibiotics, including **neomycin.**

Waksman was awarded the 1952 Nobel Prize in Physiology or Medicine for his discovery of streptomycin. He turned a large portion of the proceeds from his patents on streptomycin and neomycin, as well as the Nobel Prize money, over to Rutgers; the trustees of the University built the Institute of Microbiology and appointed Waksman its first director.

Astronomer **EDWIN POWELL HUBBLE** discovered the existence of other galaxies outside our own and provided evidence for the expanding universe. The son of a lawyer, Hubble was born in rural Missouri. He attended the University of Chicago and was awarded a Rhodes Scholarship to Oxford, England, where he earned a law degree in 1912. He returned to the United States to practice law but gave it up after only one year.

Hubble turned his attention to astronomy and, in 1914, took a research post at the University of Chicago's Yerkes Observatory in Wisconsin. When the United States entered World War I in 1917, Hubble volunteered; he completed his PhD in astronomy three days before reporting for duty.

After the war, Hubble took a position at the **Mount Wilson Observatory**, near Los Angeles, California. Hubble used the newly built 100-inch reflector to study nebulae. He detected twelve variable stars of the

Cepheid type in the great spiral nebula in Andromeda. The Cepheids had a brightness related to their period of rotation and could be used to measure distance. In 1924, he announced that the great spiral in Andromeda was a galaxy, a huge collection of stars like the Milky Way.

As he studied the light from galaxies, Hubble made another important discovery—the red shift. He found that light from the galaxies was always shifted toward the red, indicating that they were receding from the Earth. Hubble measured the speed and distance of forty-six galaxies. The most distant ones had the greatest velocity. In 1929, he announced **Hubble's law**: the greater the distance of a galaxy, the faster it is receding.

During World War II, Hubble served as a civilian doing ballistic research. He used the wartime blackout of Los Angeles to make telescopic photographs that were unhindered by the glow of city lights. After the war, he began a search for distant galaxies, using Mt. Palomar's 200-inch telescope, which he helped design. Exposures through the telescope took hours. For the most remote ones, Hubble guided the telescope throughout the night, then as morning approached, he closed the shutter to prevent fogging, and resumed the exposure the next night. One exposure lasted two weeks.

Hubble interpreted his findings to mean the universe was expanding. If the universe were expanding, then in the distant past it had a beginning, the **Big Bang**. The ratio of distance to speed of recession was called the **Hubble constant**. Its value allowed astronomers to calculate the size and age of the universe.

In 1990, the **Hubble Space Telescope** was named in his honor and built to provide a better value for the constant.

◆ Physicist **ROBERT WATSON-WATT** played a major role in the **invention of radar**. Born in Scotland, he attended the University of St. Andrews and graduated with a degree in engineering in 1912. Watson-Watt went to work for the British government in 1915 and held government posts for most of his career. In 1915, Watson-Watt served as a meteorologist at the Farnborough Royal Aircraft Factory. His assignment was to develop equipment to warn airmen of approaching thunderstorms. Scientists had noted that radio waves reflected from an electrically charged layer, the ionosphere, in the upper atmosphere of the Earth. Watson-Watt knew that thunderstorms produced ionization; he also noted that the shorter the radio waves, the more likely they were to be reflected. In 1919, he patented a device concerned with radiolocation by means of shortwave radio waves.

The equipment Watson-Watt designed sent out a pulse of very short radio waves now called **microwaves**. They reflected from the aircraft or other obstacle and bounced back to the transmitter. The difference in time between transmission and reception of the returned pulse gave the distance, or range, to the target. Radar took its name from the letters of radio detection and ranging.

In 1923, Watson-Watt conceived the idea of displaying radio information on a cathode ray oscilloscope. From the blip on the screen, the radar operator could tell the direction and distance of the target. By watching it for a few minutes, the operator could also calculate the velocity.

In 1935, Watson-Watt headed the radio department of the **National Physical Laboratory**. He drafted a report, "The Detection of Aircraft by Radio Methods," which came to the attention of a government defense committee. He was authorized to make a test by tracking a **Heyford Bomber**. Following the successful test, he was put in charge of a secret plan to build radar stations along the English coast. Completed in 1939, the stations Watson-Watt designed and installed could track aircraft at day or night and in all weather conditions.

In the early months of World War II, Watson-Watt's network of radar stations detected approaching German aircraft and plotted their positions. British fighter pilots were guided to their targets by radio. The vital information gave the **Royal Air Force** the means to successfully engage the German Messerschmitts during the **Battle of Britain** in 1940. Watson-Watt's contributions were quickly realized, and before the United States entered the war, he went there to help America complete its radar systems.

Following the war, radar developed rapidly, both for military and civilian uses. It was used for air traffic control, navigation, speed measurement, and planetary observation.

ARTHUR HOLLY COMPTON investigated the particle nature of light, discovered the nature of cosmic rays, and participated in the development of the atomic bomb. The son of a Presbyterian minister who was Dean of Wooster College in Ohio, Compton did his undergraduate work at Wooster and then earned a PhD from Princeton University in 1916. While at Princeton, Compton investigated the scattering of X-rays from crystals. He continued to work on the problem while studying under nuclear physicist **Ernest Rutherford** at Cambridge University in England in 1919, and at Washington University in St. Louis, Missouri, as head of the physics department from 1920 to 1922.

Compton bombarded crystals with X-rays. He measured the wavelength of X-rays before hitting the crystals and after being scattered by them. After scattering, the X-rays had longer wavelengths and less energy. The recoil of an electron when struck by an X-ray was clearly visible in the cloud chamber invented by Scottish physicist Charles Wilson. In 1922, Compton announced his finding, which became known as the

Compton effect: an electromagnetic wave (such as an X-ray) increases its wavelength and gives up energy when it strikes an electron. He invented the name **photon** for a bundle of light energy. Compton's discovery became an important step in **quantum mechanics** because it helped establish the particle nature of waves. In 1927, Compton shared the Nobel Prize in Physics with Wilson.

In 1923, Compton moved to the University of Chicago and remained there for more than twenty years. During the 1930s, he studied cosmic rays. Most scientists believed they were waves similar to X-rays and gamma rays, but with even higher energies. Waves would be unaffected by a magnetic field. Compton used the Earth's magnetic field to test their nature. He traveled the world, set up his instruments, and measured the rate of cosmic ray bombardment. He found that there was a latitude effect. The closer to the poles, the greater the bombardment of cosmic rays. The concentration was at the magnetic poles that were about a thousand miles from the geographic poles. He proved that cosmic rays were subatomic particles, chiefly protons, that arrived from outer space at nearly the speed of light.

During World War II, Compton administered the secret **Manhattan Project** at the University of Chicago. The project developed the first sustained and controlled nuclear reaction and built the first nuclear bombs. He directed research on breeder reactors that produced more radioactive material than they consumed. The second nuclear bomb, dropped on Nagasaki, was made from plutonium created at the Hanford, Washington, breeder reactor. After the war, Compton became chancellor of Washington University, and he remained in St. Louis after he retired.

IRÈNE JOLIOT-CURIE and her husband, Frédéric, created **artificial radioactivity** in lighter elements, a discovery that had theoretical and medical benefits. Joliot-Curie was the firstborn daughter of Pierre and Marie Curie (see no. 68). In 1914, she graduated from the College Sévigné in Gagny, France, and then entered the Sorbonne where her mother taught. During World War I, Joliot-Curie served as a nurse and operated X-ray equipment. After the war, she continued her education, and in 1925, she received her PhD in physics. She then began assisting her mother at the **Radium Institute**, where she met another assistant, Frédéric Joliot. Irène and Frédéric married in 1926. They worked together as a scientific team, jointly

signed their research papers, and both assumed the name Joliot-Curie.

In 1934, the Joliot-Curies bombarded light elements such as aluminum with alpha particles. The aluminum changed into an unstable isotope of phosphorus. After the bombardment ended, the phosphorus continued to display radioactivity. It was the first proof that radioactive elements could be artificially produced from stable elements. Lighter elements such as phosphorus are found in living tissue. Making the lighter elements radioactive made it possible to trace life processes in plants and animals. For example, the Joliot-Curies induced radioactivity in iodine. Because it was radioactive, the behavior of the iodine in the body could be traced. This showed iodine's role in the thyroid gland. In 1935, Irène and her

husband were awarded the Nobel Prize in Chemistry for the synthesis of **new radioactive elements.**

Irène and Frédéric discovered that neutrons were produced when uranium atoms split. This implied that a small trigger of a few neutrons could produce a nuclear explosion. At the time this work was completed, Nazi Germany occupied France. Until then, the Joliot-Curies had believed all scientific information should be published. Seeing the possibility of a weapon of tremendous power that might fall into Nazi hands, they chose not to report the discovery.

World War II ended scientific research in France. Irène and Frédéric managed to smuggle out the largest amount of heavy water then available. Heavy water contained hydrogen atoms with extra neutrons that were important for atomic research. Irène took her children to Switzerland in 1944, while Frédéric remained in Paris and became a leader in the national resistance movement.

After the war, Irène became a member of the Commission for Atomic Energy. She was also a member of the Communist-organized World Peace Council, and Frédéric became president of the French Communist Party. In the 1950s, they were relieved of their government posts because of their involvement in the Communist Party. In 1956, Irène died of leukemia, as her mother had, an illness that was caused by exposure to radiation. Frédéric died two years later of an illness caused by hepatitis.

LINUS PAULING was the first person to be awarded Nobel Prizes in two unrelated fields. The son of a pharmacist, as a youngster Pauling became fascinated by chemistry. After attending Oregon State Agricultural College, he received a PhD in chemistry in 1925 at the California Institute of Technology. After a short stay in Europe, he became a professor at the school, and for the next thirty-eight years he did his most important chemical work there.

Pauling pioneered the use of quantum mechanics to explain chemical bonds. He viewed electrons as waves that took their positions around the atom based on their wavelengths. Chemical bonds formed in order to make electron waves more stable. Pauling developed the **resonance theory** that showed that in some molecules, electrons could be shared by several atoms. This idea helped explain the chemical activity of circular molecules such as benzene. Pauling introduced another key chemical concept: the idea of **electronegativity**, the strength with which atoms attract electrons. His book, *The Nature of the Chemical Bond* (1939),

became one of the most important chemistry textbooks of the twentieth century.

During the 1940s, Pauling investigated molecules found in living tissue. He showed how simple amino acids, which he called the building blocks of life, linked together to give complex protein molecules. He calculated the shape of large protein molecules by how hydrogen attracted other atoms within the molecules. He showed that hydrogen bonds cause proteins to fold into the shape of a spiral staircase, or helix. This concept assisted biochemists in their understanding of the deoxyribonucleic acid (DNA) molecule.

Pauling studied the structure of hemoglobin molecules and discovered the genetic defect that causes sickle-cell anemia. In 1954, Pauling received the Nobel Prize in Chemistry for his research into the **nature of the chemical bond.**

Following World War II, Pauling became an outspoken critic of aboveground nuclear testing. He compiled scientific data detailing the harm nuclear radiation could cause and published his book *No More War!* in 1958. He drew up an appeal to end nuclear testing that was signed by more than eleven thousand scientists in forty-nine countries. His activities during this period made him quite unpopular with the U.S. government and even many of his scientific colleagues. His work did not immediately slow the arms race, though it did cause both sides to exercise more caution in nuclear testing. In 1963, the major powers signed the **Nuclear Test Ban Treaty** that outlawed aboveground nuclear tests. On the day the treaty took effect, the Nobel Committee awarded the Peace Prize to Pauling.

In 1973, Pauling founded the Linus Pauling Institute of Science and Medicine in Menlo Park, California, and served as its director until his death.

ENRICO FERMI carried out the first controlled **nuclear chain reaction**. Born in Rome, Italy, Fermi was a brilliant student and graduated from the University of Pisa, with a PhD in physics before he was twenty-one years old. In 1927, he became a full professor at the University of Rome and quickly established himself as a top-rank physicist.

Fermi applied statistical methods to explain the behavior of atomic particles. He showed that no two particles within an atom could have exactly the same properties. In 1934, he shot the recently discovered neutron into various elements. Because the neutron had no charge, it could penetrate deeper into the atom. Most researchers assumed that faster neutrons would have a greater effect.

Fermi found the reverse to be true. By sending the neutrons through paraffin, he slowed them down to the speed of molecules at room temperature. Almost every element he tested was subject to modification by slow neutrons. Absorption of neutrons by uranium atoms caused the atoms to split into roughly equal pieces, although Fermi did not recognize this at first.

During the 1930s, Benito Mussolini's fascist government implemented many repressive practices, including laws against Jews. Fermi was strongly opposed to fascism and had a Jewish wife. In 1938, he received the Nobel Prize in Physics for his discovery of nuclear reactions brought about by slow neutrons.

Fermi took his family to Stockholm to accept the prize. After the ceremony, they did not return to Italy but instead traveled to the United States, where Fermi joined the staff of Columbia University in New York.

In 1939, Fermi learned of the discovery by **Lise Meitner** (see no. 71) that uranium fission released secondary neutrons. He realized secondary neutrons could start a nuclear chain reaction with an immense release of energy. He and a coworker, Leo Szilard, composed a letter, which was signed by **Albert Einstein** (see no. 72), and delivered to President Franklin D. Roosevelt: "...extremely powerful bombs of a new type may thus be constructed." The president authorized what became known as the **Manhattan Project**, and Fermi was assigned the task of producing a controlled, self-sustaining nuclear chain reaction.

Fermi's team stacked blocks of uranium and uranium oxide as fuel, graphite as a moderator, and cadmium rods to absorb neutrons under a squash court at the University of Chicago. On December 2, 1942, only one year after he was given the assignment, Fermi had the cadmium rods slowly withdrawn. The chain reaction became self-sustaining. The success was telegraphed to Washington: "The Italian navigator has entered the new world."

Shortly before the end of the war, Fermi became a United States citizen, and in 1946, he became a professor at the University of Chicago. Element 100 was named **fermium** in his honor.

German physicist **WERNER HEISENBERG** developed quantum theory and devised the **uncertainty principle**, which concerns matter, radiation, and their reactions. Heisenberg was born in Würzburg, the son of a professor of Greek languages at the University of Munich, where young Heisenberg graduated with a PhD in physics in 1923. For the next two years, he worked with Danish physicist Niels Bohr (see no. 74) at the University of Copenhagen.

In June 1925, Heisenberg traveled to the island of Helgoland in the North Sea to relieve his hay fever. While on the island he developed a new form of quantum mechanics. He rejected the idea of collecting observations to build a picture of the atom and then developing a mathematical model to summarize the picture. Heisenberg took only the information that could be observed about the atom and expressed it in matrix mathematics to represent the atom. In 1925, he published his **theory of matrix mechanics**. His theory predicted that hydrogen gas, which is made of two hydrogen atoms, would show a dual spectrum. One would be

caused by a molecule in which the nuclei of both atoms spun in the same direction. The other molecule would have nuclei that spun in opposite directions. His prediction proved correct.

In 1927, at age twenty-six, he was appointed professor of theoretical physics at the University of Leipzig, where he remained for fourteen years. The next year he published the uncertainty principle, which states that the position and the momentum (mass times velocity) of an object cannot both be measured exactly at the same time. A more accurate measurement of one quantity causes the other one to be less precisely known. While many scientists aided in the development of quantum physics, the uncertainty principle was Heisenberg's alone.

Although it applied to all bodies, the principle became apparent only for objects smaller than the atom. The exact calculations of classical physics had to be replaced with calculations of probabilities. When trying to determine the location of a particle in an atom, the uncertainty principle challenged traditional concepts of cause and effect. **Albert Einstein** did not immediately accept the uncertainty principle and challenged its validity with thought experiments. In every test, Heisenberg or Niels Bohr, who supported the principle, were able to show errors in Einstein's assumptions. Heisenberg received the 1932 Nobel Prize in Physics for his work in quantum mechanics.

During the war years, Heisenberg stayed in Germany and worked at the Kaiser Wilhelm Institute for Physics in Berlin. For a time after World War II, he was imprisoned in England. Upon his return to Germany, he reorganized the Kaiser Wilhelm Institute as the Max Planck Institute for Physics and became its director.

MARGARET MEAD brought the study of **anthropology** to the attention of the general public. The daughter of two educators, Mead enrolled at DePauw University in 1919 with plans for a major in English. After one year, she transferred to Barnard College at Columbia University to study psychology. While there, she took a class under the well-known anthropologist Franz Boas and embraced his contention that no culture was superior to another. She rejected the idea that anthropology should be concerned with ranking cultures on a hierarchy of attainment from primitive to modern. Boas also noted that small indigenous cultures throughout the world were rapidly dying out. Mead realized if these cultures were not studied in a timely manner, the insights they held could disappear forever.

In 1925, Mead traveled to **Samoa** in the Pacific to perform original fieldwork for her doctoral dissertation. The twenty-three-year-old Mead lived on the island of Tau with an American family, the Holts. She learned the native language in six weeks and immersed herself in the Samoan culture. She focused her studies on the development of adolescent girls on the island. Shortly after her return from Samoa, Mead accepted a post at the **American Museum of Natural History** in New York. She remained with that institution for fifty-two years.

In 1928, Mead published her thesis, *Coming of Age in Samoa*, and it became a bestselling book. By the time she received her PhD in 1929, she had already become the best-known anthropologist in the United States. While other anthropologists tended to adopt a single culture and study it for their entire career, Mead visited six other cultures in the Pacific. In the late 1920s, she made a trip to **New Guinea** and examined intellectual development in young children in relation to their cultural environment. In 1930, she wrote a book about it, *Growing Up in New Guinea.*

During her life, Mead wrote forty-four books, one thousand articles, and in one expedition to Bali took 38,000 photographs. She concluded that culture rather than genetics determines variations in human behavior. She used a holistic approach in which she analyzed a culture with respect to all of its aspects, rather than a few traits that made the culture distinctive. She relied on her personal observations rather than statistical data. For that reason, some anthropologists did not wholeheartedly endorse her conclusions.

For fifty years, she was one of the best-known scientists in the United States. She wrote a monthly column for *Redbook* magazine (1961–1978) and made numerous appearances on televisions talk shows. In 1972, she recounted her early life in her book, *Blackberry Winter*. In 1974, Mead was elected president of the American Association for the Advancement of Science.

Geneticist **BARBARA McCLINTOCK** proved that genes could change position on chromosomes, one of the most important genetic discoveries of the twentieth century. McClintock was born in Hartford, Connecticut, and she studied botany at Cornell University in Ithaca, New York. In the fall of 1921, she attended a course in genetics, the only one Cornell offered to undergraduates. The next year, while still an undergraduate, she took the only other genetics course offered at Cornell, this one for graduate students. She decided to pursue an advanced degree in cytogenetics, the study of cellular components responsible for heredity. She received a PhD in 1927.

One of the goals of geneticists was to map the location of genes on a chromosome that controlled a particular trait. They believed that genes were strung together in fixed locations on the chromosome. As an undergraduate at Cornell, and later at the Carnegie Institute at Cold Spring Harbor, New York, McClintock studied the chromosomes found in maize, also known as Indian

corn. She analyzed ten chromosomes and identified genes that each one carried. These genes revealed themselves as visible traits such as the color of kernels of corn. As McClintock experimented with variations in the coloration of kernels of maize, she discovered that the traits did not remain in the same location. Some genes could jump from one place to another in a chromosome, or from one chromosome to another.

In 1951, she reported that genetic information could transpose from one chromosome to another. Other scientists did not accept this capability of genes, and the importance of her work was not immediately recognized. During the next twenty years, her additional studies, as well as confirmation from independent sources, showed that genes could change position. In 1983, she received the Nobel Prize in Physiology or Medicine for her discovery of mobile genetic elements.

Newspapers used the phrase "jumping genes" to report about her work, although geneticists used the term **"transposons."** Scientists found transposons in every species, not just maize. McClintock's discovery that genes are not stable had enormous implications and overturned one of the main theories of heredity laid down by **Gregor Mendel** (see no. 48). For example, scientists suspected that the transposed genes might make bacteria resistant to antibiotics, cause some normal cells to transform into cancerous ones, and lead to rapid changes in a species by mutation. A transposon of genetic material in human chromosomes was found to be the cause of chronic myelogenic leukemia.

By the time of her death at age ninety, McClintock's work was generally considered to rank with that of Mendel's original discovery of the laws of dominant and recessive genes.

GRACE BREWSTER MURRAY was born in New York City. As a young girl, she showed a strong interest in gadgets. Alarm clocks were not safe in her house because she took them apart to see how they worked! Murray attended Vassar College, where she received her degree in mathematics and physics. While teaching at Vassar she continued her studies at Yale and in 1934, earned a PhD. She married Vincent Foster Hopper in 1930. They later divorced, and she never remarried.

During World War II, she was admitted to the navy reserves. After finishing at the top of her midshipman's class, Lieutenant Hopper was assigned to Commander Howard Aiken at Harvard University to assist him as he built the **first large-scale computer**. Completed in 1944, the **Mark I** was fifty-one feet long, eight feet high, and weighed thirty-five tons. It was a hybrid mechanical-electronic computer designed to calculate firing angles for naval guns. Hopper became one of the three programmers for Mark I.

After the war, she remained at Harvard in the computer laboratory. One day, when the new Mark II computer shut down, she traced the reason to a moth that had flown through an open window and into one of the mechanical relays. She reported the incident and taped the bug into the logbook. From then on, when her team had to find a problem, they described it as "debugging" the system. In 1949, she joined the John Eckert-Mauchly Computer Corporation (later Unisys) as senior mathematician. The company produced **UNIVAC**, a commercial computer for business tasks such as billing and payroll. On the night of the presidential election of 1952, with only 7 percent of the returns available, UNIVAC correctly predicted that Dwight David Eisenhower would win the election.

Hopper was one of the first people to realize that programming languages should be written for people who were neither mathematicians nor computer experts. In 1956, she developed the FLOW-MATIC compiler that had near English-like statements. Hopper helped formulate the specifications for **COBOL**, the common oriented business language. She developed validation tests to confirm that COBOL compilers worked properly. The concept of validation became an important step to certify computer software.

Hopper was a tireless speaker and teacher. In 1966, she retired from the navy, but the next year they recalled her to active duty to standardize payroll software. In 1969, the Data Processing Management Association created the Computer Science Man-of-the-Year Award. Hopper was the first person to receive it. In 1986 at age seventy-nine, she retired from the navy with the rank of rear admiral, the oldest officer on active duty. When she died in 1992, she was buried with full military honors at Arlington National Cemetery.

Physicist **MARIE GOEPPERT-MAYER** developed a theory that explained why some atomic nuclei are more stable than others. Her theory laid the groundwork for later development in nuclear physics.

Born in Kattowitz, Prussia (now Katowice, Poland), Goeppert came from a long line of university professors. When she was four years old, her father became a professor at the University of Göttingen. In 1924, she enrolled at that university with the intention of becoming a mathematician. However, the theoretical physicist **Max Born** guided her scientific education toward physics. In 1930, she received her PhD at the University of Göttingen in theoretical physics. Her thesis involved calculating the changes in the state of electrons under the rules of quantum mechanics.

Goeppert married American chemist **Joseph Edward Mayer**, whom she met at Göttingen, and in 1933 she went with him to the United States to Johns Hopkins University in Baltimore. It was in the midst of the Depression, and Goeppert-Mayer could find no professional appointment. So,

she worked at the university without pay or formal academic standing. She applied quantum mechanics to chemistry and had ten research papers published by 1939. In 1940, she and her husband wrote *Statistical Mechanics*, a textbook that remained in print for more than forty years.

During World War II, while her husband was at Columbia University, she worked for American chemist Harold Urey in developing ways to separate isotopes of uranium. In 1946, she and her husband moved to the University of Chicago. She continued to hold informal positions, although she gained a part-time federal grant as the senior physicist at the Argonne National Laboratory. At the time she and her husband went there, the University of Chicago was the center of nuclear research in an academic setting. She met Edward Teller and Enrico Fermi, and both scientists encouraged her as she took up the question of **nuclear structure.**

Goeppert-Mayer developed the concept that protons and neutrons in the nucleus arranged themselves in shells, similar to the shells of electrons around the nucleus. Nuclei with complete shells were more stable than those nuclei with incomplete shells. A German physicist, **Hans Daniel Jensen** (1907–1973), had arrived at a similar notion. When she learned of his independent discovery, she contacted him, and in 1955, they coauthored a book on the subject, *Elementary Theory of Nuclear Shell Structure*.

In 1960, Goeppert-Mayer moved to the University of California at San Diego, and for the first time had a full-time faculty appointment. In 1963, she and Jensen received the Nobel Prize in Physics for their development of nuclear shell structures. She was the second woman to receive the Nobel Prize in Physics. Marie Goeppert-Mayer died in 1972 after a series of strokes.

JOHN BARDEEN was a two-time Nobel Prize winner in physics who helped develop transistors and made advances in superconductivity. Born in Madison, Wisconsin, Bardeen studied electrical engineering at the University of Wisconsin. He studied advanced mathematics and physics at Princeton University, where he received a PhD in 1936. After teaching at the University of Minnesota for three years, Bardeen served as a civilian physicist with the Naval Ordnance Laboratory in Washington, DC, throughout World War II.

After the war, Bardeen joined Bell Telephone Laboratories in New Jersey, where he remained until 1951. At Bell Telephone, he worked with William B. Shockley (see no. 88) and Walter H. Brattain. On December 16, 1947, while experimenting with coatings on the surface of a germanium crystal, they connected it to two wires a small distance apart. A small power gain occurred, amplifying a voice signal forty times. In January 1948, they announced the **discovery of the transistor.**

Compared to vacuum tubes, transistors used less power, generated far less heat, required no warm-up time, and could withstand jolts and other rough treatment. In addition, they could be built smaller than vacuum tubes. Transistors found their first use in hearing aids made small enough to fit in the ear. As cost decreased, transistors were used in calculators and computers. The first vacuum tube computers were so large they took up entire floors of buildings. By the late 1960s, the use of transistors reduced the size of computers to cabinets that took up one wall of a room. By the end of the 1970s, the cabinet-sized calculating machine had become a desktop computer. Bardeen, Shockley, and Brattain shared the Nobel Prize in Physics in 1956 for their work on semiconductors and their discovery of the transistor effect.

In 1951, Bardeen moved to the University of Illinois, where he revisited earlier work he had once done on electrical conductivity. At a few degrees above absolute zero, most metals lost their electrical resistance and became superconductors. This effect had been observed in 1911 in mercury, but no one had succeeded in providing an explanation.

Bardeen showed that at the extremely cold temperatures, the metals formed a solid lattice. Electrons coupled with each other with a force that overcame the disruption caused by motion due to heat. Bardeen and two graduate students, Leon Cooper and J. Robert Schrieffer, developed the **first successful theory of superconductivity**. They named it the BCS theory (their initials) and announced it in 1957. In 1972 the three men received the Nobel Prize in Physics for their jointly developed theory of superconductivity.

WILLIAM SHOCKLEY co-invented the transistor and helped shape its role in the advancement of electronics. Born in London to American parents, Shockley was raised in Palo Alto, California. In 1932, he earned an undergraduate degree from the California Institute of Technology and, in 1936, received a PhD in solid-state physics from the Massachusetts Institute of Technology. After graduation, he joined Bell Telephone Laboratories in Murray Hill, New Jersey. At Bell, he experimented with the electrical conductivity of germanium and silicon crystals. The elements were known as semiconductors because they were intermediate in their electrical conductivity between metals and nonmetals.

During World War II, Shockley directed antisubmarine research for the U.S. Navy. After the war, he returned to Bell Laboratories as director of research into solid-state physics. Working with **John Bardeen** (see no. 87) and **Walter Brattain,** he resumed attempts to use semiconductors to amplify and control electronic signals. The three researchers found that adding certain impurities, such as arsenic or boron, to the semiconductor crystals resulted in an excess or deficit of electrons in the regular lattice of the crystal. The presence of extra electrons—or absence of electrons—modified the regular matrix of the crystal. The impurities affected the way electric current moved through the crystal.

The three scientists invented the point-contact transistor in 1947, although it was not announced until the following year. In 1948, they built a more effective device, the junction transistor. The devices were called transistors because they transferred current across a semiconductor resistor. In 1956, Shockley, Bardeen, and Brattain received the Nobel Prize in Physics for their research on semiconductors and their **invention of the transistor**. Shockley continued to research applications of the transistor. In 1955, he resigned his position at Bell Laboratories to become Director of the Shockley Semiconductor Laboratory in Mountain View, California. He received more than fifty patents for new transistor and semiconductor devices. Other high-tech companies were located near his facility. The region at the southern end of San Francisco Bay became known as **Silicon Valley**. Beginning in 1958, Shockley lectured at Stanford University, and in 1963, he became professor of engineering science.

During the 1970s, Shockley generated considerable controversy when he began to express his views on genetics. He publicly stated **his theory that intelligence is genetically based**, and that Black people were genetically inferior to whites in terms of intelligence. This was greeted by a storm of disapproval. Some scientists abandoned their association with him. They pointed out that he was working outside his field of expertise.

After his retirement in 1974, Shockley lived at his home on the campus of Stanford University. There he continued to develop his controversial opinions on the relationship of race to intelligence.

Biochemist **DOROTHY CROWFOOT HODGKIN** used X-ray techniques to analyze the structure of penicillin, insulin, and vitamin B_{12}. The daughter of an archaeologist, she was born in Cairo, Egypt, where her father worked at the Egyptian Ministry of Education. She attended school in England and, in 1932, completed her undergraduate work at Somerville College, Oxford. In 1937, she received a PhD from Cambridge University.

At Cambridge, she was introduced to the technique of X-ray diffraction to show the structure of crystals. Waves that strike crystals are bent as they pass through small openings or around obstructions. The waves change direction and interfere with one another. The diffraction pattern reveals how the atoms of a compound are situated in the crystal. The compound to be tested is reduced to a crystal, and then the X-ray diffraction pattern photographed and measured. Her doctoral thesis was based on her X-ray diffraction study of the digestive enzyme pepsin.

After graduation, Hodgkin returned to Somerville College at Oxford to continue her research work. In 1937, she began to use X-ray diffraction to investigate insulin, a hormone that regulates the metabolism of the body. Until that time, only simpler non-organic compounds were subjected to X-ray studies. Organic compounds were highly complicated. While her studies of insulin were incomplete at the start of World War II, she shifted her investigation to the important antibiotic penicillin. Knowledge of its structure would make possible widespread manufacture of the drug in great quantities and at reduced cost.

Because of the complexity of the molecule, she abandoned pen-and-paper calculations in favor of processing by electronic computer. By 1945, she succeeded in completely determining the **atomic structure of penicillin**. In 1947, the Royal Society recognized her achievements by electing her a member.

Hodgkin had an informal team of researchers who assisted her in her research. Some of them were students, and others were visitors from various universities. Beginning in 1948, she started work on analyzing vitamin B_{12}. It was a complex molecule four times the size of penicillin, and once again, she used a computer to aid in detailing its structure. By 1955, she had established the locations of the atoms that composed it. In 1964, Hodgkin was awarded the Nobel Prize in Chemistry for her determination of the structures of important biochemical substances by X-ray techniques.

During this time, Hodgkin had continued to study insulin, a complex protein. In 1953, English biochemist **Frederick Sanger** (see no. 94) determined its composition, and Hodgkin produced a three-dimensional picture of its structure in 1969.

In 1970, Hodgkin became Chancellor of Bristol University and helped found a Hodgkin scholarship for students from the developing world. In 1977, she became president of the British Association for the Advancement of Science.

JACQUES YVES COUSTEAU was a French oceanographer who opened the undersea world to exploration by both scientists and the general public. Cousteau was not formally trained as a scientist. He graduated from France's Brest Naval Academy in 1933 and was commissioned as a second lieutenant. He was to begin training as a navy pilot but suffered severe injuries in an automobile accident. Part of his physical therapy for recovery included swimming. He took up diving and became fascinated with undersea exploration. At the time, the only diving equipment available was a compressed air cylinder that restricted divers to short periods of time beneath the surface. Cousteau began to test new diving equipment that would enable divers to stay underwater for longer periods.

During World War II, Cousteau met **Émile Gagnan**, an expert on industrial gas equipment. Together they developed and tested a cylinder of compressed air connected through a pressure-regulating valve to a face mask—a self-contained air lung. With this device, the **aqualung**, a diver could breathe underwater without a clumsy diving suit. The device was self-contained and did not require a lifeline that connected a diver to the surface. It enabled people to dive to great depths and remain beneath the surface for longer periods. The device also became known as scuba gear. Successfully used in 1943, the apparatus became commercially available in 1946.

In 1945, Cousteau founded the French Navy's Undersea Research Group. In 1950, he became the commander of the *Calypso*, a British minesweeper that he converted into an oceanographic research vessel. In 1953, he published *The Silent World*, a book about life beneath the sea. He also experimented with **underwater filmmaking** and developed housings for underwater cameras. In 1956, he resigned from the navy with the rank of captain. He produced a documentary titled *The Silent World*, and it won the Academy Award for Best Documentary of 1957.

Cousteau became director of the Oceanographic Museum of Monaco in 1957. He designed structures for living underwater for prolonged periods. The documentary *World Without Sun* (1964) about those experiments below the Red Sea earned him another Academy Award. In addition to diving apparatus, habitats, and underwater camera housings, Cousteau also invented the diving **saucer**—a small, easily controlled submarine.

Part of Cousteau's **worldwide exploration of the oceans** was funded by a highly popular television series he narrated and produced, *The Undersea World of Jacques Cousteau* (1968–1976); it became one of the most popular shows on American television. The *Calypso* served as Cousteau's floating laboratory until it sank in 1996. Cousteau died in 1997; at the time of his death, he was raising money to outfit a replacement vessel, *Calypso II*.

◆ **LUIS ALVAREZ** studied short-lived subatomic particles and helped popularize the theory that a giant meteorite crashed into the Earth millions of years ago and killed the dinosaurs. Alvarez was born in San Francisco and earned a PhD in physics from the University of Chicago in 1936. As a member of the faculty of the University of California, Berkeley, he discovered a form of radiation that occurred when the nucleus of an atom captured the innermost electron of the atom.

During World War II, Alvarez worked on the U.S. atom bomb project at Chicago and at Los Alamos, New Mexico, for two years. On July 16, 1945, he witnessed the atomic bomb test at Trinity Site near Alamogordo, New Mexico. On August 6, 1945, Alvarez flew as a scientific observer in a B-29 that accompanied the *Enola Gay* that dropped the atomic bomb on Hiroshima, Japan.

After World War II, Alvarez returned to Berkeley, where he studied short-lived subatomic particles that were created by a linear accelerator of his design. To detect particles, Alvarez built a large bubble chamber containing pure liquid hydrogen at –270 degrees Celsius. Hydrogen consisted of a single proton, which made identification of reactions simpler. Particles passing through the liquid created a string of bubbles along their track, which were then photographed and studied. A million photographs of nuclear events were taken the first year. Alvarez built automated equipment to scan the photographs and pass the information to a computer for analysis. His methods revealed a large number of previously unknown fundamental particles. In 1968, Alvarez received the Nobel Prize in Physics for his contribution to elementary particle physics and his technique of using the **hydrogen bubble chamber.**

In 1979, Luis and his son, Walter Alvarez, made an announcement that captured the imagination of people all over the world. Walter Alvarez—a geology professor—was doing research in Bubbio, Italy, when he noted a layer of sediment about an inch thick. When his father analyzed the sediment, he found it contained an unusually high concentration of iridium, an element that is common in meteorites but rare on Earth. The iridium-rich layer—later found in several other places across the Earth—dated from 65 million years ago, at the end of the **Cretaceous** period when the dinosaurs died. Father and son developed a theory that **a giant meteorite impact** caused the mass extinction of dinosaurs. They speculated that the impact produced a dust cloud that obscured the Sun for three years, plunging the Earth into a long winter that reduced vegetation and caused the death of larger animals. Scientists eventually came to widely accept at least the first part of the theory.

Physicist **CHARLES HARD TOWNES** did the fundamental work that led to the construction of the laser. The son of a lawyer, Townes grew up in Greenville, South Carolina. He attended Furman University, pursued double degrees—in physics and modern languages—and graduated summa cum laude at the age of nineteen. In 1939, he received a PhD from the California Institute of Technology.

During World War II, Townes worked on radar systems for Bell Laboratories. In 1950, he moved to Columbia University, where he made his most important discovery. Because of his radar research, he recognized the need for a device to generate high-intensity microwaves. However, no electronic circuit was capable of creating the waves. He knew that heat or electricity would give ammonia molecules the energy to release microwaves. A small beam of microwaves sent through ammonia gas would stimulate the molecules to release their energy at the same time. Even a feeble beam would start the process. The slight cascade would grow

into an avalanche. The result would be a flood of microwaves all of the same wavelength and in step with one another.

In December 1953, Townes and his students constructed such a device. It became known as a **maser**, taking the initials from microwave amplification by stimulated emission of radiation. The regular vibration of ammonia molecules as revealed by the microwaves made it possible to control a clock with unprecedented precision. Townes built an improved maser based on solids rather than gases. The solid-state masers introduced a minimum of noise, while amplifying extremely faint radio signals. Signals from spacecraft deep in space could be received and understood.

In 1958, Townes and his brother-in-law, **Arthur Leonard Schawlow**, advanced the possibility of a visible light maser, a **laser**. Two years later, Stanford University physicist **Theodore Harold Maiman** built a ruby laser rod. After strobe lights pumped energy into the rod, laser light broke out in a tight parallel bundle with all the waves of the same frequency. Concentrating the rays still tighter by a lens produced enormous power in a confined area. Because of their higher frequency, laser light waves were capable of carrying a hundred thousand times more information than microwaves.

In 1961, Townes moved to the Massachusetts Institute of Technology and was working there in 1964 when he received the Nobel Prize in Physics for his fundamental work that led to the construction of masers and lasers. He shared the prize with two Russian scientists who had done similar, but not as well-publicized, work. In 1967, Townes went to the University of California at Berkeley to head a program of radio and infrared astronomy. He retired in 1986 and remained professor emeritus until his death in 2015.

Physicist **RICHARD FEYNMAN** developed a highly accurate physical theory about nuclear interactions. Feynman was born in New York City and studied physics at the Massachusetts Institute of Technology. In 1942, he received a PhD from Princeton University. During World War II, he worked at Los Alamos, New Mexico, and devised the formula to predict the energy yield of nuclear bombs.

After the war, Feynman worked at Cornell University, where he tackled the perplexing problem of how electrons interacted with the electromagnetic fields that their motions created. The quantum electrodynamics theory then in use had defects that caused some calculations to become infinite and therefore useless. Nuclear weapons were being based on a theory that failed at key calculations.

Feynman created a new method of expressing **quantum electrodynamics**. He introduced graphical pictures, called **Feynman diagrams**, that made the complicated study far easier to comprehend. His results agreed with experimental tests to an accuracy never before achieved by a scientific theory. In 1965, he shared the Nobel Prize in Physics with two other scientists for fundamental work in quantum electrodynamics.

In 1950, Feynman settled permanently at the California Institute of Technology. He applied quantum mechanics to explain superfluidity, a state of matter near absolute zero in which liquid helium flows with no resistance. He also worked on weak interaction forces and strong forces. Weak interaction was a type of radioactive decay in which electrons were emitted from the nucleus of the atom. Strong forces held the nucleus together despite the powerful electrical repulsion among protons. This study convinced him that protons and neutrons were made of still smaller particles, later called quarks.

In 1986, Feynman was appointed to the Rogers Commission to investigate the *Challenger* space shuttle explosion that killed seven astronauts. He became frustrated with the slow pace of the investigation and the vague, bureaucratic answers. During a live broadcast, he soaked an O-ring seal in ice water and showed how its loss of resiliency caused the leak that was responsible for the explosion.

Feynman was renowned for his excellence as a lecturer. His three-volume collection, *The Feynman Lectures on Physics* (1965), became a classic. The book was illustrated with a photograph showing him playing bongo drums, an attempt to put a human face to science. He also published two volumes of autobiography, *Surely You're Joking, Mr. Feynman!* (1984), and *What Do You Care What Other People Think?* (1988). During his career, Feynman enjoyed informally meeting with high school physics students, and lamented the fact that after he won the Nobel Prize, the schools usually put him in the auditorium to lecture to the entire student body. He taught until two weeks before his death in 1988.

English biochemist **FREDERICK SANGER** developed methods to reveal the sequence of amino acids in complex protein molecules and was the first person to map a complete DNA molecule. Sanger's father, a physician, influenced him to enter a career in science. At first, he studied for medicine but realized his temperament was better suited for long-term projects rather than the daily distractions of a medical practice. Sanger entered graduate school at Cambridge University in 1939 and became fascinated by the substances found in living organisms. In 1943, he graduated with a PhD in biochemistry. He then remained at Cambridge and worked and studied there for the next forty years.

In his work, Sanger developed methods to determine the **structure of proteins**. For his study, Sanger chose insulin, a protein hormone produced in the pancreas that regulates metabolism. By treating an insulin molecule with a mild acid, he separated it into two chains. One chain had thirty-one amino acids and the other had twenty. Sulfur atoms bridged across the chains

and held them together. Sanger broke the chains into smaller fragments to learn the sequence of the amino acids on each chain. In one experiment, he treated the insulin with weaker acids and obtained fragments that he separated by paper chromatography. The amino acid segments flowed down a vertical strip of paper and each one dropped out at a specific location.

In another method, Sanger treated the pieces with a dye molecule. The colored marker, which he had discovered, attached itself to one end of the smaller chains but not the other. He then broke the fragments down completely by boiling them in strong acid. He found the terminal components by their colors. Sanger reconstructed first one chain, and then the other, from the pieces he had identified. By 1953, he had worked out the complete sequence of amino acids in insulin. In 1958, Sanger received the Nobel Prize in Chemistry for his work on the structure of proteins.

The recognition of the Nobel Prize helped Sanger obtain improved research facilities and gave him the confidence to attack a still more difficult problem. He tackled the intricate sequencing of nucleotides in deoxyribonucleic acid, DNA. He investigated the DNA molecule of a bacterial virus that contained 5,375 pairs of nucleotides. Each nucleotide contained one of four smaller molecules called bases. By 1977, he had succeeded in determining the exact sequence of the bases throughout the DNA. The methods he devised were used to map the organization of DNA in humans. In 1980, Sanger shared the Nobel Prize in Chemistry with two U.S. scientists who had performed similar work on the **structure and function of DNA**. With this award, Sanger became the first person to be awarded a Nobel Prize in Chemistry twice. He retired in 1983.

Biophysicist **ROSALIND FRANKLIN** played an essential role in the "race to the double-helix"—the discovery of the structure of DNA, the molecule that encodes genetic information. In 1941, Franklin received a degree in chemistry from Newnham College at Cambridge University; she continued her education at Cambridge and received her PhD in 1945. Following World War II, she worked in Paris at the State Chemical Laboratory, where she learned X-ray diffraction techniques.

In 1950, Franklin took a position at the Biophysical Laboratory, King's College, part of the University of London. Her supervisor, James Randall, gave her the task of deciphering the structure of the complex DNA molecule. Despite poor equipment, Franklin invented a way to produce **high-resolution X-ray diffraction** photographs of the molecule. Her photographs indicated that the DNA molecule has a double spiral structure, a double helix. She also calculated the location of the important chemical groups along the strands. Franklin was not convinced that the DNA had a double helix structure under all conditions and insisted on making additional tests.

Franklin's X-ray diffraction photographs came to the attention of **Maurice Wilkins**, a coworker. Wilkins showed the photographs to **James Watson** (see no. 99) and **Francis Crick** without her knowledge. They used the photographs to confirm their own double helix structure of the DNA molecule. The paper Watson and Crick published in 1953 in the science journal *Nature* made no mention of the assistance they received from Franklin.

In 1953, Franklin switched affiliation to Bierkbeck College. In the college's crystallography laboratory, she finished her work on the DNA molecule and went on to study the tobacco mosaic virus.

She established that the ribonucleic acid of the virus, RNA, was a single helix. She then took up a highly dangerous study of live poliovirus. In 1958, Franklin's promising scientific career was cut short when she died of ovarian cancer. She was only thirty-seven years old.

In 1962, Watson, Crick, and Wilkins shared the Nobel Prize in Physiology or Medicine for their decoding of the DNA molecule. Franklin was ineligible because the award was given only to living individuals. However, even had she lived, it is doubtful she would have received a share of the award at that time. Her work had been portrayed as only a footnote to the accomplishments of Watson and Crick. At the Nobel ceremony, no official acknowledgment was made of her contribution to the discovery.

By the end of the century, however, Franklin's X-ray diffraction photographs, the skill with which she made them, and her interpretation of the results had become better known. The reevaluation of her contributions gave Franklin a greater share of the credit for the discovery of the DNA structure.

ROSALYN SUSSMAN YALOW was a medical physicist who developed an extremely sensitive technique for detecting minute quantities of hormones present in the body. Born Rosalyn Sussman to immigrant parents who had no high school education, Yalow became interested in physics while attending Hunter College in New York City. As a young woman, she read Eve Curie's biography of her famous mother, Marie Curie, and heard Enrico Fermi when he spoke at her college in 1939. After she graduated in 1941, she received a teaching assistant position in physics at the University of Illinois–Urbana Champaign. She was the only woman among four hundred members of the College of Engineering.

At the university she met **Aaron Yalow**, a graduate physics student, and they were married in 1943. In 1945, she graduated with a PhD in nuclear physics and returned to Hunter College to teach. Because of her interest in medicine, she volunteered to work at a medical laboratory in the Bronx. This led to a part-time position in 1947 with the Bronx Veterans Administration Hospital. In 1950, she left teaching to become a full-time medical researcher at the hospital. There she collaborated with **Solomon A. Berson**, a medical doctor, in the application of radioisotopes to measuring contents of blood and other body fluids.

In her work, Yalow noticed that when a patient was treated with animal insulin, the patient's body created antibodies that removed the insulin. Antibodies are proteins that chemically nullify invaders by binding with them and changing their chemical characteristics. In attempting to measure changes in the amount of insulin, Yalow and Berson **developed radioimmunoassay**, RIA.

They began by binding an antibody with a radioactive sample of insulin. A small sample of blood containing the insulin to be measured was mixed with the preparation. Some of the antibody switched from the radioactive insulin to the blood insulin. The decrease in binding of antibodies to radioactive insulin could be measured, and its decrease was proportional to the total amount of regular insulin in the blood.

RIA applied to other substances besides insulin. It could measure minute amounts of biological substances such as enzymes, hormones, steroids, and vitamins in blood and other body fluids. The technique made possible detailed measurements of chemicals that would have escaped detection by any other method. RIA could identify concentrations of one picogram per milliliter (1.0 thousand-billionth gram per milliliter).

From 1956 to 1960, Yalow and Berson published papers about their discovery. Although incredibly sensitive, the procedure was straightforward and could be carried out in hospitals around the world, even primitive ones in developing countries. Berson died in 1972. In 1977, Yalow shared the Nobel Prize in Physiology or Medicine for her development of RIA, making her the first American-born woman to win a Nobel Prize in a scientific field. In 1988, she received the National Medal of Science, and in 1993, she was inducted into the National Women's Hall of Fame.

HAR GOBIND KHORANA is credited with cracking the genetic code that controls the production of protein in cells. Khorana was born of Hindu parents in a small village in India, and attended Punjab University in Lahore (now Pakistan). After earning his master's degree in 1945, he received a government fellowship to study at the University of Liverpool in England, where he received his PhD in 1948. Over the next several years, he studied and performed research in Switzerland, England, and Vancouver, British Columbia. In 1960, Khorana moved to the Enzyme Institute at the University of Wisconsin, where he did some of his most important work. While there, he also became a United States citizen.

In the early 1960s, Khorana experimented with unraveling the genetic code, the process that deoxyribonucleic acid, DNA, uses to instruct cells to produce a particular protein. (In addition to heredity information, DNA also contains instructions for the daily functioning of cells.) DNA produced molecules of ribonucleic acid (RNA) that carried instructions to the cells encoded as a series of nucleotides, sometimes called nucleic acids. Khorana proved that each instruction on the RNA molecule was a group of three nucleotides. Each three-nucleotide code stood for a specific amino acid. The cells read the code, made amino acids, and put them together to produce protein. Khorana also identified the three-letter nucleotide start and stop sequence that instructed the cell when to start reading the RNA and when to stop reading it.

Khorana determined the sequence of DNA nucleotide triples that code the twenty amino acids. He succeeded in synthesizing small nucleotide molecules and combined them with the raw chemicals they needed to produce synthetic amino acids identical to those produced in living cells.

One result of his research was that, with only a few exceptions, the same nucleotide code produced the same amino acid in all species. By **unraveling the genetic code** for one species, the results could be applied to all living organisms. In 1968, Khorana shared the Nobel Prize in Physiology or Medicine for his interpretation of the genetic code.

In 1970, Khorana prepared the **first artificial copy of a gene**, one of yeast. He also worked out the techniques to put together nucleotide triplets in ways that did not exist in nature. This made it possible to substitute synthetic sequences onto a gene that existed in nature to genetically alter the function of the gene. His work started the biotechnology industry of gene-altered plants and foods.

In 1970, Khorana became professor of biology and chemistry at the Massachusetts Institute of Technology. In 1996, he found that misformed proteins in certain cells of the eye may be responsible for the form of blindness known as retinitis pigmentosa.

TSUNG-DAO LEE overthrew a well-regarded theory of physics that had guided nuclear research for more than thirty years. Lee was born in Shanghai, China, and began college there. After World War II, he emigrated to the United States, and enrolled at the University of Chicago, where he was accepted as a PhD candidate. In Chicago, he worked under nuclear physicist Enrico Fermi and received his PhD in 1950. The following year, he accepted a fellowship for research at the Institute of Advanced Study at Princeton, New Jersey.

At Princeton, Lee renewed his acquaintance with **Chen Ning Yang**, a fellow Chinese scientist. In 1953, Lee became a professor at Columbia University in New York City. He and Yang continued to hold weekly meetings. Their work involved elementary particle physics—the study of the most minute particles of matter. They worked on the puzzling problem of the theta-meson and tau-meson decay. The theta-meson and tau-meson particles decayed in different ways, but otherwise appeared to have

identical properties. Lee would have concluded that the two mesons were the same particle, but to do so would have violated a law of elementary particle physics—the law of conservation of parity.

The law of conservation of parity stated that nuclear reactions always took place in such a way as to not reveal whether the observer was looking at them directly or in a mirror. According to parity, no reaction would permit a distinction between right and left. If the theta- and tau-mesons were the same particle, then Lee would be able to tell left from right by the way the single particle broke down. Lee tried to bring his understanding of the meson reactions in line with the conservation of parity. Finally, Lee inquired as to what experimental evidence supported the law of conservation of parity. He was astonished to learn that no such experimental evidence existed. A law of physics had been established based on theoretical considerations without any data to support the theory.

Lee and Yang devised a number of experiments to test the asymmetry in particle physics. Both of them were theoretical physicists, so they appealed to an experimental physicist, **Chien-Shiung Wu**, to carry out the experiments. Wu tested the proposal in 1956 by observing beta particles (electrons) given off by cobalt-60. She used radioactive cobalt held in a magnetic field. According to parity, as many electrons should have been emitted in the up direction as in the down direction. However, more electrons from the radioactive process were emitted downward than upward. It was a stunning discovery because physicists had always found nature symmetric. The validity of the **overthrow of parity** was so convincing that in Lee and Yang were awarded the Nobel Prize in Physics in 1957.

JAMES DEWEY WATSON identified the double helix nature of deoxyribonucleic acid, DNA, and explained its crucial role in carrying **genetic traits**. Born in Chicago, Watson entered the University of Chicago at age fifteen and earned a PhD in zoology at the University of Indiana at age twenty-two. After graduation, Watson received a grant to study the effects of radiation on viruses at the University of Copenhagen in Denmark. However, after meeting Cambridge researcher Maurice Wilkins at a seminar in Naples, Italy, Watson became convinced that a more important research topic was the significance of DNA in genetics.

In 1951, Watson transferred to the Cavendish Laboratory at Cambridge University in England. There he met **Francis Crick**, who had been attempting to solve the structure of DNA. Crick's model did not meet the experimental evidence, nor did it embody the information partially revealed by X-ray diffraction photographs. The problem was to explain how a DNA molecule could replicate, or copy, itself during cell division. Watson began constructing a three-dimensional physical model. He knew DNA was a helix, a spiral shape, and he had the breakthrough idea that it was a **double helix**, with the important nucleic acids, or nucleotides, arranged as steps between the rails. He showed that only four different nucleotides existed, and each step was a pair of nucleotides. Along the DNA molecule, a vast amount of heredity information was encoded in the millions of nucleotide steps.

Watson's physical model agreed with the experimental data. It explained how the DNA molecule could copy itself by splitting down the middle, with each complementary helix serving as a pattern to rebuild a duplicate of the original. Although half of the molecule was missing, the chemical nature of the existing part forced an exact copy of the missing part. In 1953, Watson and Crick published their model in the science journal *Nature*. Waston returned to the United States, spent two years at the California Institute of Technology, and then moved to Harvard University in 1956. In 1962, Watson shared with Crick and Wilkins the Nobel Prize in Physiology or Medicine.

In 1968, Watson published his book *The Double Helix*, a subjective account of the DNA research. The book became a bestseller and created controversy because of Watson's candid opinions, especially an unflattering portrait of **Rosalind Franklin** (see no. 95), who made some of the X-ray photographs that guided his work.

In 1968, Watson moved to the Quantitative Biology Laboratory at Cold Spring Harbor in New York, which he headed for twenty years. From 1988 to 1992, he worked at the National Institutes of Health as head of the **Human Genome Project**, an ambitious effort to map the entire sequence of human DNA, which was completed in 2003. In 2007, Watson published his fully sequenced genome online, becoming only the second person to do so.

1942–2018

Physicist **STEPHEN HAWKING** combined the theory of relativity with quantum mechanics to describe the **properties of black holes**. Hawking was born in Oxford, England. Although he could not read until he was eight years old and was only a lackluster student, Hawking decided to pursue a career in cosmology, the study of the universe at large. He attended Cambridge University, and shortly after his twenty-first birthday, he was **diagnosed with amyotrophic lateral sclerosis**, ALS, known in the United States as Lou Gehrig's disease. Doctors could offer no cure or treatment. Despite the setback, he continued to pursue his studies and received his PhD in 1966.

In his research, Hawking investigated black holes, objects far denser than anything previously studied in physics. Black holes are formed by massive stars that exhaust their nuclear fuel and collapse to a point of zero volume and infinite density. Escape velocity in a black hole is greater than the speed of light, so black holes can be detected only by their gravitational effects on nearby objects.

Physicists had no mathematics to deal with matter in this condition. Hawking realized that because of their large mass, Einstein's theory of relativity had to be used, but because of their tiny size, black holes also followed the rules of quantum mechanics.

Hawking pointed out that mini black holes could have been produced at the time of the **Big Bang**, scientists' term for when the universe was created. In 1974, his studies showed that energy could escape from black holes. Smaller black holes could evaporate,

and the process was so rapid that they might explode and emit particles in the form of thermal radiation—the so-called **Hawking radiation**.

Hawking never again saw the doctor who diagnosed his disease and offered no hope. Instead, his father, a medical researcher, became his chief medical adviser. By 1974, his condition required more assistance than his wife could provide. For six years, he was assisted by research students, and in 1980, he began to rely on nurses. By 1986, he needed twenty-four-hour nursing care. His condition had progressed so that he was incapable of speech or free movement.

Despite being mobile only with the aid of a wheelchair and speaking with a computer-aided voice synthesizer, Hawking traveled widely, delivered speeches to large audiences, and continued to write. His book, *A Brief History of Time*, published in 1988, gives a popular account of cosmology, and became an international bestseller.

In 1979, Cambridge awarded Hawking the Lucasian professorship of mathematics, a post held by Isaac Newton three hundred years earlier. During the 1990s and 2000s, Hawking continued his work in physics and continued writing for wide audiences, including *A Briefer History of Time*, which he published in 2005, and several children's books coauthored with his daughter, Lucy. He died in March of 2018, and his final paper was published posthumously in April 2018.

TRIVIA QUESTIONS

Test your knowledge and challenge your friends with the following questions. The answers are contained in the biographies noted.

1. Which famous ancient Greek person is known as the father of medicine? (See no. 2)

2. Which ancient Greek physician studied the dissected dead bodies of animals to draw his conclusions about the anatomy of humans? (See no. 7)

3. Who first put forth the theory that the Earth moves around the Sun, and not the other way around? (See no. 9)

4. Why was a seventeenth-century scientist tried and convicted of heresy and sentenced to house arrest? (See no. 11)

5. Which Dutch scientist made more than four hundred microscopes during his lifetime? (See no. 18)

6. Which American scientist helped draft the Declaration of Independence and was one of its signatories? (See no. 23)

7. Why was a famous French scientist tried, convicted, and executed during the French Revolution? (See no. 29)

8. How did the uneducated son of a poor London blacksmith learn enough science to become a famous chemist? (See no. 39)

9. Which nineteenth-century American naval officer devised a system of recording oceanographic data that is still in use today? (See no. 42)

10. Where did a famous English scientist find evidence that led him to produce his theory that humans probably evolved from an earlier, subhuman form? (See no. 44)

11. Why is a nineteenth-century English countess called the first computer programmer? (See no. 45)

12. Where did a famous American inventor establish the first U.S. research laboratory? (See no. 57)

13. Which Austrian doctor originated the theory of psychoanalysis and believed that a person's unconscious mind influences their behavior? (See no. 64)

14. Who was born into slavery and went on to become one of the world's greatest plant scientists? (See no. 67)

15. Who is recognized as the greatest scientist of the twentieth century? (See no. 72)

16. How did a French oceanographer help finance his worldwide exploration of the oceans? (See no. 90)

PROJECT SUGGESTIONS

1. Choose one of the scientists from this book and write a fictional diary entry for one day in that person's life. Pick a day that had some significance for the individual; for example, the day he or she made an important discovery or scientific breakthrough, or the day he or she was awarded the Nobel Prize. Or choose a day on which the person was frustrated by a lack of success in solving a scientific problem. Describe the person's thoughts and feelings with as much detail as you can.

2. What do you think is the most important scientific discovery or advancement of the past one hundred years? Write a brief essay telling the reasons for your choice; include why you think this discovery has made life better for society, and why life might be more difficult for people if it had not occurred.

INDEX

OUT NOW:

100 African Americans Who Shaped American History

100 American Women Who Shaped American History

100 Americans Who Shaped American History

100 Artists Who Shaped World History

100 Athletes Who Shaped Sports History

100 Authors Who Shaped World History

100 Baseball Legends Who Shaped Sports History

100 Battles That Shaped World History

100 Books That Shaped World History

100 Colonial Leaders Who Shaped World History

100 Disasters That Shaped World History

100 Events That Shaped World History

100 Explorers Who Shaped World History

100 Families Who Shaped World History

100 Folk Heroes Who Shaped World History

100 Great Cities of World History

100 Hispanic and Latino Americans Who Shaped American History

100 Immigrants Who Shaped American History

100 Inventions That Shaped World History

100 Medical Milestones That Shaped World History

100 Men Who Shaped World History

100 Military Leaders Who Shaped World History

100 Native Americans Who Shaped American History

100 Natural Wonders of the World

100 Relationships That Shaped World History

100 Ships and Planes That Shaped World History

100 Spiritual Leaders Who Shaped World History

100 Wars That Shaped World History

100 Women Who Shaped World History

100 World Leaders Who Shaped World History